First World War
and Army of Occupation
War Diary
France, Belgium and Germany

25 DIVISION
75 Infantry Brigade
Cheshire Regiment
11th Battalion
25 September 1915 - 31 July 1918

WO95/2250/1

The Naval & Military Press Ltd
www.nmarchive.com
Published in association with The National Archives

Published by

The Naval & Military Press Ltd

Unit 10 Ridgewood Industrial Park,

Uckfield, East Sussex,

TN22 5QE England

Tel: +44 (0) 1825 749494

www.naval-military-press.com

www.nmarchive.com

This diary has been reprinted in facsimile from the original. Any imperfections are inevitably reproduced and the quality may fall short of modern type and cartographic standards.

© **Crown Copyright**
Images reproduced by permission of The National Archives, London, England, 2015.

Contents

Document type	Place/Title	Date From	Date To
Heading	11th Bn Cheshire Regt Sep 1915-Jly 1918 Disbanded Aug 3-1918		
Heading	25th Division 11th Cheshire Vol I Sept & Oct 15 Jly 18		
War Diary	Aldershot	25/09/1915	25/09/1915
War Diary	Southampton	26/09/1915	26/09/1915
War Diary	Havre	26/09/1915	27/09/1915
War Diary	Caestre	28/09/1915	28/09/1915
War Diary	Oosterove Farm	28/09/1915	03/10/1915
War Diary	Ploegsteert Wood	04/10/1915	21/10/1915
War Diary	Hants Fm	22/10/1915	24/10/1915
War Diary	Ploegsteert Wood	25/10/1915	01/11/1915
Heading	25th Division 11th Cheshire Rgt Vol 2 Nov 15 & Dec		
Heading	25th Div 11th Cheshire Vol 3		
War Diary	Hants Fm	01/11/1915	04/11/1915
War Diary	Ploegsteert Wood	04/11/1915	14/11/1915
War Diary	Ploegsteert Wood T113-120 (inclusive)	15/11/1915	20/11/1915
War Diary	Ploegsteert Wood	21/11/1915	22/11/1915
War Diary	Subsidiary Line 1009 Sheet	23/11/1915	25/11/1915
War Diary	Ploegsteert Wood	26/11/1915	26/11/1915
War Diary	Subsidiary Line	27/11/1915	27/11/1915
War Diary	T. 113-120	27/11/1915	28/11/1915
War Diary	Ploegsteert Wood T113-120 (inclusive)	29/11/1915	02/12/1915
War Diary	Creslow	03/12/1915	04/12/1915
War Diary	Ploegsteert Creslow	05/12/1915	06/12/1915
War Diary	T 113-125 (inclusive)	07/12/1915	08/12/1915
War Diary	Ploegsteert Wood T113-120 (inclusive)	08/12/1915	13/12/1915
War Diary	Creslow	13/12/1915	14/12/1915
War Diary	T 113-120 (inclusive)	17/12/1915	18/12/1915
War Diary	Ploegsteert Wood T113-120 (inclusive)	19/12/1915	23/12/1915
War Diary	Ploegsteert Wood Creslow (billets) T113-120 (inclusive)	24/12/1915	28/12/1915
War Diary	Ploegsteert Wood T113-120 (inclusive)	28/12/1915	31/12/1915
Heading	11th Battn. Cheshire Regiment. January 1916		
War Diary	Ploegsteert Wood	01/01/1916	01/01/1916
War Diary	Creslow (billets)	01/01/1916	06/01/1916
War Diary	Ploegsteert Wood	06/01/1916	11/01/1916
War Diary	Creslow	12/01/1916	12/01/1916
War Diary	Creslow (billets)	12/01/1916	19/01/1916
War Diary	Ploegsteert Wood	19/01/1916	23/01/1916
War Diary	Ploegsteert Wood T113-120 (inclusive)	23/01/1916	23/01/1916
War Diary	Brigade Reserve	24/01/1916	26/01/1916
War Diary	La Creche	26/01/1916	26/01/1916
War Diary	Strazeele	27/01/1916	31/01/1916
Heading	11th Battn. Cheshire Regiment. February 1916		
War Diary		05/02/1916	08/02/1916
War Diary	Strazeele	09/02/1916	26/02/1916
War Diary	Strazeele	13/02/1916	13/02/1916
Heading	11th Battn. Cheshire Regiment. March 1916		
War Diary	Strazeele	04/03/1916	10/03/1916
War Diary	Nedonchelle	11/03/1916	11/03/1916
War Diary	Valhuon	16/03/1916	25/03/1916

Type	Location	Start	End
War Diary	Tinques	24/03/1916	31/03/1916
Heading	11th Battn. Cheshire Regiment. 1st To 19th April 1916		
Heading	War Diary Of 11th (S) Batt. Cheshire Regiment. From 1-4-16 To 3-6-16		
War Diary	Tinques	01/04/1916	04/04/1916
War Diary	Chelers	12/04/1916	19/04/1916
Heading	11th Battn. Cheshire Regiment. 20th April to 1st June 1916.		
War Diary		20/04/1916	20/04/1916
War Diary	Btn H.Q. Neuville St Vaaste Front Line	27/04/1916	27/04/1916
War Diary	Ecoivres	06/05/1916	08/05/1916
War Diary	Neuville Saint Vaaste	09/05/1916	11/05/1916
War Diary	Neville St Vaaste Bde Reserve	19/05/1916	19/05/1916
War Diary	Neuville	19/05/1916	19/05/1916
War Diary	Front Line	20/05/1916	21/05/1916
War Diary	Ecoivres	26/05/1916	26/05/1916
War Diary	Mingoval	01/06/1916	01/06/1916
Heading	11th Battn. Cheshire Regiment. 3rd to 30th June. 1916.		
War Diary	Tinques	05/05/1916	09/06/1916
War Diary	Mingoval	03/06/1916	09/06/1916
War Diary	Mowtes En Terwois	14/06/1916	14/06/1916
War Diary	Villers D'Hopital	15/06/1916	17/06/1916
War Diary	Bernaville	18/06/1916	18/06/1916
War Diary	St. Duen	19/06/1916	24/06/1916
War Diary	Thalmas	25/06/1916	27/06/1916
War Diary	Toutencourt	29/06/1916	30/06/1916
Heading	11th Battalion The Cheshire Regiment. July 1916		
War Diary	Hedauville	01/07/1916	01/07/1916
Miscellaneous			
War Diary			
War Diary	Thiepval	03/07/1916	04/07/1916
War Diary	Albert	05/07/1916	07/07/1916
War Diary	Ovillers	08/07/1916	22/07/1916
War Diary	Mailly-Maillet	31/07/1916	31/07/1916
Miscellaneous	A Form. Messages And Signals.	04/07/1916	04/17/1916
Miscellaneous	A Form. Messages And Signals.		
Heading	75th Brigade. 25th Division. 1/11th Battalion Cheshire Regiment August 1916		
War Diary	Mailly Maillet	01/08/1916	10/08/1916
War Diary	Bois-de-Warnimont	11/08/1916	15/08/1916
War Diary	Raincheval		
War Diary	Forceville	17/08/1916	19/08/1916
War Diary	Aveluy Wood		
War Diary	Authville Wood	22/08/1916	22/08/1916
Heading	11th. Cheshire Regt. September 1916.		
Miscellaneous	A Form. Messages And Signals.	31/08/1916	31/08/1916
War Diary	Authville	01/09/1916	03/09/1916
War Diary	Authville Wood	04/09/1916	12/09/1916
War Diary	Agenville	12/09/1916	29/09/1916
Heading	11th Battn. Cheshire Regiment. October 1916.		
War Diary	Aveluy	01/10/1916	04/10/1916
War Diary	In Trenches	05/10/1916	06/10/1916
War Diary	Ovillers Post	07/10/1916	14/10/1916
War Diary	Trenches	15/10/1916	22/10/1916
War Diary	Warloy	23/10/1916	23/10/1916
War Diary	Authieule	24/10/1916	31/10/1916

Heading	11th Battn. Cheshire Regiment. November 1916.		
War Diary	Meteren	01/11/1916	26/11/1916
Heading	11th Battn. Cheshire Regiment. December, 1916.		
War Diary		01/12/1916	26/12/1916
War Diary	Ploegsteert	01/01/1917	02/01/1917
War Diary	Nieppe	03/01/1917	16/01/1917
War Diary	Le Touquet	17/01/1917	22/01/1917
War Diary	Le Bizet	23/01/1917	23/01/1917
War Diary	Le Touquet	29/01/1917	29/01/1917
Miscellaneous	A Form. Messages And Signals.	01/01/1917	01/01/1917
War Diary	Le Touquet	01/02/1917	01/02/1917
War Diary	Pont De Nieppe	04/02/1917	04/02/1917
War Diary	Le Bizet	08/02/1917	08/02/1917
War Diary	Le Touquet	10/02/1917	16/02/1917
War Diary	Le Bizet	16/02/1917	18/02/1917
War Diary	Le Touquet	22/02/1917	22/02/1917
War Diary	Nieppe	25/02/1917	25/02/1917
War Diary	Godewaersvelde	26/02/1917	01/03/1917
War Diary	Renescure	13/03/1917	13/03/1917
War Diary	West Becourt	14/03/1917	14/03/1917
War Diary	Etrehem	20/03/1917	20/03/1917
War Diary	Sercus	21/03/1917	21/03/1917
War Diary	Grand Sec Bois	22/03/1917	22/03/1917
War Diary	Outtersteene	24/03/1917	01/04/1917
War Diary	Neuve Eglise	04/04/1917	04/04/1917
War Diary	Steenwerck	13/04/1917	13/04/1917
War Diary	Le Bizet	20/04/1917	20/04/1917
War Diary	Le Touquet	25/04/1917	25/04/1917
War Diary	Erquinghem	29/04/1917	29/04/1917
War Diary	Outtersteene	30/04/1917	01/05/1917
War Diary	St Marie Cappel	08/05/1917	08/05/1917
War Diary	La Creche	15/05/1917	15/05/1917
War Diary	Ravelsburg	29/05/1917	31/05/1917
Heading	War Diary of 11th (S). Battalion Cheshire Rgt. for the month of June 1917.		
War Diary	Ravelsburg	01/06/1917	01/06/1917
War Diary	Neuve Eglise-Dranoutre Wood	03/06/1917	08/06/1917
War Diary	Neuve Eglise	09/06/1917	11/06/1917
War Diary	Trenches E. of Messines	12/06/1917	15/06/1917
War Diary	Pioneer Camp	17/06/1917	17/06/1917
War Diary	Sec Bois	24/06/1917	24/06/1917
War Diary	Merville	25/06/1917	25/06/1917
War Diary	St. Hilaire	26/06/1917	26/06/1917
War Diary	Reclinghem	27/06/1917	01/07/1917
War Diary	Thiennes	08/07/1917	08/07/1917
War Diary	Dominion Camp	09/07/1917	09/07/1917
War Diary	Camp At Sheet 27 L.17.a.9.8	22/07/1917	31/07/1917
War Diary	Westhoek Ridge	01/08/1917	01/08/1917
War Diary	Ypres	06/08/1917	09/08/1917
War Diary	Halifax Camp.	09/08/1917	09/08/1917
War Diary	Westhoek Ridge	11/08/1917	13/08/1917
War Diary	Dominion Camp.	16/08/1917	16/08/1917
War Diary	Ypres	16/08/1917	17/08/1917
War Diary	Godewaersvelde	18/08/1917	18/08/1917
War Diary	Steenvoorde	20/08/1917	01/09/1917
War Diary	Dominion Camp	02/09/1917	02/09/1917

War Diary	Dickebusch	03/09/1917	03/09/1917
War Diary	Halfway Ho	05/09/1917	05/09/1917
War Diary	Dickebusch	09/09/1917	09/09/1917
War Diary	Halifax Camp	10/09/1917	10/09/1917
War Diary	Caestre	12/09/1917	12/09/1917
War Diary	Thiennes	13/09/1917	13/09/1917
War Diary	Allouagne	14/09/1917	26/09/1917
War Diary	Noeux Les Mines	27/09/1917	27/09/1917
War Diary	Cite St Pierre	28/09/1917	01/10/1917
War Diary	Les Brebis	04/10/1917	04/10/1917
War Diary	Vaudricourt	05/10/1917	05/10/1917
War Diary	Front Line (Canal Sector)	06/10/1917	06/10/1917
War Diary	Le Preol	12/10/1917	12/10/1917
War Diary	Front Line	18/10/1917	18/10/1917
War Diary	Support	24/10/1917	24/10/1917
War Diary	Front Line	30/10/1917	30/10/1917
War Diary			
War Diary	Canal Right Sector	01/11/1917	01/11/1917
War Diary	Le Preol	05/11/1917	05/11/1917
War Diary	Canal Right Sector	11/11/1917	16/11/1917
War Diary	Pontfixe	17/11/1917	22/11/1917
War Diary	Canal Right Sector	23/11/1917	27/11/1917
War Diary	Bethune	28/11/1917	28/11/1917
War Diary	Bas Rieux	29/11/1917	29/11/1917
War Diary	Laires	30/11/1917	05/12/1917
War Diary	Rocquigny	05/12/1917	09/12/1917
War Diary	Bapaume	09/12/1917	16/12/1917
War Diary	Favreuil	16/12/1917	31/12/1917
War Diary	Lagnicourt Trenches	01/01/1918	01/01/1918
War Diary	Favreuil	02/01/1918	04/01/1918
War Diary	Vaulx	14/01/1918	14/01/1918
War Diary	Lagnicourt Trenches	20/01/1918	21/01/1918
War Diary	Favreuil	26/01/1918	06/02/1918
War Diary	Lagnicourt	07/02/1918	07/02/1918
War Diary	Favreuil	12/02/1918	12/02/1918
War Diary	Logeast Wood	13/02/1918	14/02/1918
Heading	11th Battalion Cheshire Regiment March 1918		
Miscellaneous	75th Infantry Brigade	05/04/1918	05/04/1918
War Diary	Logeast Camp	01/03/1918	07/03/1918
War Diary	Berkeley Camp	12/03/1918	12/03/1918
War Diary	Bihucourt	13/03/1918	13/03/1918
War Diary	Berkeley Camp Bihucourt G.12.c.5.3. No. 11 Camp Favreuil H. 12 Central	21/03/1918	21/03/1918
War Diary	I. 10 Central	22/03/1918	22/03/1918
War Diary	I. 12.a.9.7	22/03/1918	22/03/1918
War Diary	I. 17.a.5.8	22/03/1918	22/03/1918
War Diary	I. 12.a.9.7	22/03/1918	22/03/1918
War Diary	I. 17.a.5.8	22/03/1918	23/03/1918
War Diary	G. 22.d.	23/03/1918	23/03/1918
War Diary	Sapignies	24/03/1918	24/03/1918
War Diary	Logeast Wood	25/03/1918	25/03/1918
War Diary	Puisieux	25/03/1918	26/03/1918
War Diary	Gommecourt	26/03/1918	31/03/1918
War Diary			
Heading	11th Battalion The Cheshire Regiment April 1918		
War Diary		01/04/1918	19/04/1918

War Diary	R.27.a.5.2	20/04/1918	31/05/1918
Miscellaneous	11/Cheshire May 1918	05/05/1931	05/05/1931
War Diary		01/06/1918	31/07/1918

25TH DIVISION
75TH INFY BDE

11TH BN CHESHIRE REGT
SEP 1915 – JLY 1918

Disbanded Aug 3 - 1918

11th Cheshires
Vol I

121/7761

15/25th Warwar

Sep 1 & Oct 15

12 sheets

Army Form C. 2118.

WAR DIARY
of
INTELLIGENCE SUMMARY.
(Erase heading not required.)

XI (S) Bn Cheshire Regiment

Instructions regarding War Diaries and Intelligence Summaries are contained in F. S. Regs. Part II. and the Staff Manual respectively. Title pages will be prepared in manuscript.

Places	Date	Hour	Summary of Events and Information	Remarks and references to Appendices
Aldershot	25-9-15	9 a.m.	The Battalion entrained at Farnboro' Station to Avonmouth, in three trains, commencing at 9 a.m. the 3rd being detrained on the Transport "Mona Queen" which sailed from Seaforth Quays for at 6 p.m. – Total strength of Battalion 1031. The ship was very crowded the men carrying all their equipment including marching blankets. The Battalion disembarked at Havre, 2nd & R.E. R.E.A. – The photographs might not be obtained with the ship.	Est.
Southampton	"			
Havre	26-9-15	7 a.m.	The Battalion entrained at Havre 400 of the R.E.A. – Transports with the ship arrived and hospital. The Battalion & men of the Battalion proceeded by way of Louvain Abbeville marched to No Rest Camp – Dispatched in obtaining arms & completed Supplies incl home trucks – Distribution, which was originally difficult.	Est.
"	27-9-15	7 a.m.	The Battalion entrained at the front did No. and detailed and left Havre, complete with transport at 2 p.m., the men travelling in home trucks – Distribution, which was originally difficult, was changed during journey, not so spent in train – journey very uncomfortable. Army rations for several meals via arrival were organised by the Railway Transport Staff.	Est.
Caestre	28-9-15	9 a.m.	The Battalion detrained and marched, advance party first, to Strazeele, whence it proceeded in motor lorries via Bailleul to Outtersteene Farm & went into billets. The transport (1st journey), 16 farm wagons, was completed in billets Abbeville, thence had been made for detrainment of horses. On arrival and ET farms it was found that the arrangements had been made for detrainment of billets. It was met the advance officers. That Mr. Rhea was nearly the work being carried out at about 11 p.m. The least of the First Reinforcement, numbering 1 noted and 1 lantern, [?] arrived & was delayed by the weather which had shot of the roads they however secured a good supply of and were quartered by themselves. No blame could be attributed to anybody, as the absence of arrangements making not sudden allocation of arms in the Battalion of the Battalion.	Est.
Outtersteene Farm	"			
"	29-9-15		The day was employed in general organisation and cleaning up of the new billets. Weather still bad; rain wet unpleasant.	Est.
"		10 a.m.	Company Commanders and 1st Platoon Commanders went into the trenches in the Ploegsteert sector to the & stay for two mechanical purposes.	
"		5.30 p.m.	Three Platoons went into the trenches for 24 hours were schooled by the 14th Canadian Infantry, to whom they were attached for instruction.	
"	30-9-15	9.30 a.m.	Fort Water. The Commanding Officer, accompanied by the Brigade Major, made a tour of the trenches of trenches N-2 – M.E. of PLOEGSTEERT WOOD, whilst the Battalion were engaged on relieving the 14th Canadian Infantry. He found the trenches muddy but fair [?] dry, having in many places a wood flooring. Traps were sunk, the shelving being much on our side – D Camp and huts into the trenches in the evening – heavy boughs made by our battle into the neighbourhood of our billets continued the greater part of the day. Several aeroplanes were over and on & none of the enemy came over & were heavily shelled with shrapnel by apparent artillery. – The G.O.C. Brigade visited the billets during the morning.	Est.
"	1-10-15	10-1.5 a.m.	2nd in Command and Adjutant & Mr. Swann Sergt went into the trenches for a day & night, in order to obtain all necessary information as to the details of daily routine. Shown over the whole line by the Commanding, and have minutely into all details of routine &c. Three most platoons were into the trenches in the evening for two further [?] inspected a portion of the line before [?]entered in the evening and found from sides to a tower and occupants. Commdrs - Report made by Brigade 1st & [?] also are arranging for R.E. to repair wire.	Est.

2353 Wt. W2544/1454 700,000 5/15 D. D. & L. A.D.S.S./Forms/C. 2118.

WAR DIARY

INTELLIGENCE SUMMARY.

Army Form C. 2118.

Instructions regarding War Diaries and Intelligence Summaries are contained in F.S. Regs., Part II. and the Staff Manual respectively. Title pages will be prepared in manuscript.

X 1st (S) Bn Wiltshire Regt.

Place	Date	Hour	Summary of Events and Information	Remarks and references to Appendices
Oosttavern Farm	2.10.15	5 a.m.	Battalion sustained first casualty, Pte. Sloan "B" Company being shot in the head by a sniper + killed almost instantaneously. 2nd in Command of Battalion relieved from trenches 11 a.m. — C.O. attended a conference of Commanders held by G.O.C. 2nd Army Corps (Maj. Paulkensson) at 11:30 p.m.	E84
"	3.10.15	9 a.m.	Relief made by the Bn. 28th F. Division, who comprised the 1st Battalion our Rice Clearly Connection 1st Battalion relieved being at 3–4.5 p.m. and 2nd in Command + Section at 2nd Trench Line in the evening of PLOEGSTEERT WOOD. Retiring 1st + 1st Canadian Infantry. The relief was uneventful + all companies being completed by 10 p.m. 3½ kls line — a good deal of Sniping during the night. The Enemy sustained doubtless supposed C.B. made over of Wood line.	E83
Ploegsteert Wood	4.10.15	9.30 a.m.	C.O. + 2 in Command inspected Communication trenches in rear of Trench line. In afternoon C.O. inspected Road to Gun Shed Trenches within altitude repairs required. Some firing from Snipers.	E83
"	5.10.15	2.0 p.m.	Lt. Col. 2nd Army Corps accompanied by the Brigadier made a tour of the Trenches — Weather very wet. A few enemy Shells came over the Trenches. Enemy firing fairly quiet.	E83
"	6.10.15	10.0 a.m.	C.O. accompanied the Brigadier on a tour of the Farm + dugouts in Battalion Reserve. Heavy artillery, ours and the armed Trenches. Sergeant of patrol found farms in hand reports. A practical of sniping during the night. Especially in front of our right. During the day. Several J.C. Sniper in front of front line No.113 at one time. One sniper shot. Shot that J.C. Enemy. One additional skilled snipers of position shown after snipers. Enemy artillery fire trench at 7 p.m. an enemy Machine Gun was heard opposite T.113. Some J.R. Brigade M.G. notified by telephone. Patrols sent out during night reported without incident except one Machine gun opened fire on working party at 11.30 a.m. with no effect. Much Sniping during night.	E83
"	7.10.15		This position taken by Battery during the day. During evening enemy fixed an additional opposite T.120 and T.130 and lodged by rifle fire and passed to Cellar. Four Central position to oppose T.113. In Brigade mid 15 Trenches of T.118.	E83
"	8.10.15	6.30 a.m. 10.30 a.m.	During the Battery relieved the Infantry was alarming — A officer. Sniper and nine Cellar. Enemy very quiet during the day.	E84
"		8.17 p.m.	Picket party fired from the Shell Battalion + 2.5 p.m.	

3353 Wt. W2544/1454 700,000 5/15 D. D. & L. A.D.S.S./Forms/C. 2118.

Army Form C. 2118.

WAR DIARY
INTELLIGENCE SUMMARY
(Erase heading not required.)

Instructions regarding War Diaries and Intelligence Summaries are contained in F.S. Regs., Part II. and the Staff Manual respectively. Title pages will be prepared in manuscript.

XIth (S) Bn Cheshire Regt.

Place	Date	Hour	Summary of Events and Information	Remarks and references to Appendices
Ploegsteert Wood	9.10.15		Wire opposite PICKET HOUSE during night of 8/9th. About a party of enemy observed working in trenches opposite T.114 -	Ext. 1
		6.30am	Working party located in BIRDCAGE. 4 rifle grenades fired by us, + our artillery opened fire on it party.	
		6 p.m.	The Battalion was relieved at 6 p.m. by 1/5. B^{n} South Lanc^{s}. The relief was completed in one hour and a half. Headquarters moved into HANTS FARM, with "A" Company remaining. The Companies were "B" Company at TOUQUET BERTHE and "C" Company in huts + tents in the W. of PLOEGSTEERT WOOD. The Battalion to be in Brigade Reserve.	
		10 p.m.	A man in "C" Company was wounded in the leg by a stopping bullet shortly after the Company had arrived at another Bivouac.	
	10.10.15		Billets had been left in a filthy condition by the previous Battalion, and the greater part of the morning was devoted to cleaning up. O.C. compared notes at 8.8. South Lancs on the question of working parties etc., to put us and protection through approaching Trenches. It was decided that in future two working parties - C.O. Hdqrs. Camp and Commanders have to supply the Working Parties required, when allotted to Companies, then Sub. Sections.	Ext. 2
		6 p.m.	Enemy aeroplane came over into British front, bombarded by shrapnel, but managed to get away.	
	11.10.15		Usual routine during morning. In afternoon O.C. held conference with Company Commanders + the O.C./R.E. on repair of Breastworks. Arrangements made for the men to have their dinners + wash before parade at LePelzeur at 8pm + dinners at 12 noon G/2 R. Lys is used for the purpose. C.O. + some men to drive to repaired enemy entrance approachable.	
	12.10.15		Battalion exercises chiefly consisted of Field Works by Companies. A Class for N.C.O's instruction lectures of lectures held under the Senior Major + R.S.M. A good deal of enemy shelling during afternoon. Whizbangs/Minies shot heavy bombard'd at Batt. Headquarters about dusk. The enemy opened fire with a machine gun, but our Lewis Guns replied. No further damage done.	
	13.10.15	1.15 am	Army Corps order received ordering "Stand to arms" one hour before dawn. Companies ordered at "Stand to arms" - localities of all - Troops were distributed as follows. Localities set well - of whole discussion of Trenches, + Hampshire Farm. Local Reserve was one farm in front of PLOEGSTEERT, and M.O. Have a line around PLOEGSTEERT for the purpose of holding front of the British were.	
		1.30 pm	Admiral Sir H. Jackson was Minister and C.O. PLOEGSTEERT WOOD. He is Inspector the Battalion Workshops. Still memory this farm after the next turn into the Trenches. The Battalion sent of Hay Stacks a heavy transport wagon load placed with a view to	

2353 Wt. W2544/1454 700,000 5/15 D.D. & L. A.D.S.S./Forms/C. 2118.

Army Form C. 2118.

WAR DIARY
INTELLIGENCE SUMMARY.
(Erase heading not required.)

X1 # (3) Bn Machine Gun

Place	Date	Hour	Summary of Events and Information	Remarks and references to Appendices
Ploegsteert Wood	13.10.15		Working at enemy's power-lift and wire entanglements. The Bonn Sand bazaar ? was [illegible] this [illegible].	[illeg.]
		7 p.m.	Enemy's guns reported but this fire was extremely desultory and did no harm. Troops returned to Billets.	
Ploegsteert Wood	14.10.15		C.O. presented & Reviewed "a" Company Transport Camp - Sergt Major held an enquiry re actions [illegible] for promotion. Several Jims were enquired for Lewis Guns as result fell. Battalion relieved & billeted. This was in "B" Company, since left by Sharm Godfroy - Battalion summary acquitted - Several casualties of a similar nature occurred since it's relief. Battalion has been in Reserve and it is supposed the Sana Sort of practice? should be erected behind the huts in the District Lines.	[illeg.]
	15.10.15		Morning Spent in several cleaning-up operations. Weather rather inclement - Officers of Pl & S. Lancaster Co. inspected all billets & latrines. In the afternoon the Battalion relieved the Pt S. Lancs in the Trenches, taking over the same section as in the previous tour. The relief was completed by 7 p.m.	
		9 p.m.	C.O. made an inspection of Trenches.	
	16.10.15	9.15 a.m.	Two of enemy seen to pass by Fresnoy? opposite junction of T118 & T117, apparently carrying food. Fired on. One fell.	
		11 a.m.	Two others seen near the dug-out at C.7. from BIRDCAGE. Several considerable parties of enemy carrying things and fired at from snipers.	
		6 p.m.	Enemy worked a fresh opposite T113. Could hear them on ramming? & taking nails in head. Men seen in grey overcoat.	
		7 p.m.	Sergt Godfroy enquired from T113 & observed a after "J. Briest" and J. Riep moving from a point about 30 yards front of PICKET HOUSE to exhaust enemy - line probably Platoon or further back - 2 Lt Sims Coy covered a point and 3 men of enemy seen - 2 repeated rack by one or other 3. Rest near Trapped. Rest sit up & climbed aright.	
		8.30 p.m.	Day seen as about 100 yards behind our support, searching the ammunition dump the Staff of mules alarmed, also heard at breath ravine.	
	17.10.15	5 p.m.	Several enemy observed flitting near READING HALL in our front line.	
		11 a.m.	Enemy working party seen opposite T110 and fired on. Also Scout croft was running across angle of enemy.	
			Statin opposite T117 as if mending line for telegraph. Brigade on that Relieves having issued Ch supplied the demolished village of LE GHEER. Good water supply discovered in old R.E. mined houses.	
		11.30 a.m.	Enemy working party seen in front T120 - Many Allications noted in enemy's trenches on Echo faint. Fired	
		10.30 p.m.	T.120, also one opposite T.119. Rockets of every sort in evening, finales.	
	8 p.m.	Brisk rifle fire on enemy's ? T113 collapse and also Part of L-Ringed of small communications trench.	[illeg.]

Army Form C. 2118.

WAR DIARY

INTELLIGENCE SUMMARY.

(Erase heading not required.)

Instructions regarding War Diaries and Intelligence Summaries are contained in F.S. Regs., Part II. and the Staff Manual respectively. Title pages will be prepared in manuscript.

X1/5(3) Bn Cheshire Regt.

Place	Date	Hour	Summary of Events and Information	Remarks and references to Appendices
Ploegsteert Wood	7-10-15		A brass cap of enemy's shell picked up near READINGHALL, markings 17 05 GT, also a brass fuse on back 52.16 M. NK cap plo marked M/V.	Est
"	16.10.15	1.30am	Patrol sent out opposite T.117 from T.119 meaning miniature Etreux; picketed - also firing from the trenches set	
		5.15am	white dog seen in wood behind M.34 at same as the 9CCN in enemy's trenches	
		10.45am	Enemy stopped support line trench under fire, pickets with Brodrick hat Balaclava, tweed & brown caps seen by [illegible]	
		10am	Our gun enemy observed at mining party, with red and khaki brass & caps. An enemy party observed at work in[?] front of enemy's trench. Enemy believed to be building another trench opposite T.117. Is building operation seen opposite T.117 in front of enemy's trench numerous scouts opposite T.119. Our gunnery opened fire & parachute observed dim & bundles carried behind party seen wearing khaki cap. An object resembling a parachute observed above a selector scout balloon behind the enemy lines opposite T.117. Enemy working party observed opposite T.120	
		2.30pm	Red & white seen up by enemy opposite T.113.	Est
		9.30pm	Capt Hughes & Sergt Grayson Went out from listening post opposite PICKET HOUSE along a ditch & reached a point within about 30 yards of enemy's lines.	
		10pm	Two men were observed over wire, but we were unable to open fire on them owing to patrol being out - our machine gun opened fire on a working party opposite T.113. Enemy attempted to enemy bombarded TOURQUET BERTHE FARM and parts of PLOEGSTEERT WOOD was shrapnel and left shrapnel	
"	17.10.15	2am	Patrol located enemy working parties digging a ditch. Works are being laid opposite T.117-117.	Est
		3.30am	White dog seen - S.T.117 followed to PALK VILLA	
		5am	White dog again seen in S.T.119, but succeeded in evading capture.	
		2.3pm	Carrier pigeon plus enemy Enemy's trench opposite T.117. Subsequent to patrol carrying cement opposite T.117 appeared moving windward.	
		4.15pm	Patrol report enemy to the trees are upper strength being numerous on at route. Some shelling during the day, own shells falling near enemy's parapet opposite T.130. A new snip out post being made behind T.119 in a ruined house. Sniping upon this all morning from Tg 999 is as far as the red J huge through barbed wire, some yellow. The lane picked is sniped at. Is Sniping upon their line. Several reports enemy being seen to have a shoulder & most of the enemy. The man was observed wearing his uniform with a round blue cap. Some Vickers fire was used of protection of 1 during the night. Two orderlies hide orders of a self-visited in the trenches during the afternoon, their snipers not proving satisfied.	Est

Army Form C. 2118.

WAR DIARY
or
INTELLIGENCE SUMMARY.

(Erase heading not required.)

X1st (S) Bn Cheshire Regt

Place	Date	Hour	Summary of Events and Information	Remarks and references to Appendices
Ploegsteert Wood	19.10.15	10.30pm	Enemy heard working on his wire. Patrols out all night confirm statement that enemy is busy strengthening his defences. Bitch being made in front of his trenches, white dog seen from T.118 during night. Some shelling occurred from both sides, our shells falling near enemy trenches at trench 123. Enemy seem to have READING HALL FORT marked. Cap is on shell which fell near marked Dopp Z 96 m/H Kr. Cap aluminum, centre brass.	N.8.K.
	20.10.15	9.15am	Working party of enemy heard using shovels & mallets. During night enemy revised 10' of his parapet by 3 sandbags. New loophole discovered (opp. T.117) again at 3.30 p.m. (opp T.117) Enemy fired with white cap band over enemy's parapet (opp. T. 116). [some time] No damage	
		10 a.m	Three rifle grenades fired at T. 113.	
		2-4pm	PICQUET HOUSE was sniped heavily all day by sniper on 118.	
		4.30pm	German sniper caught mounting a tree and shot by sniper. But enemy did not fire nor flare (for some time) — Sentry reported two men near our wire not confirmed.	
		midnight.	A few rounds chopped by our artillery on trench opp 121. REGENT ST →	A.D.K.
			Enemy quiet on the whole. white dog again seen by S. Lewis desultory 3 days in succession — Enemy out at 10 p.m. returns at 5-6 a.m.	
	21.10.15		Enemy very quiet all day but important no sign of enemy work on his own defences At 8pm Artillery of enemy trenches opp. 119, 120. Two loopholes located. A few shells fired by our artillery. Battalion was relieved in trenches round afternoon by 8th Loyal, and returned to billets at HANTS FM. Surrounding farms worked & peasants undamaged by Adjutant. re suspected sniper at PLOEGSTEERT WOOD at angle of REGENT ST and MESSINES RD	A.D.K.
HANTS FM	22.10.15	10.0am	C.O. visited proposed new billets behind (no report sand 24) several shells Day fairly quiet till afternoon when enemy dropped much less sniping at night, otherwise quiet. into LE BISET, between 4 & 5 p.m.	A.D.K. A.D.K.
	23.10.15	11 a.m	Enemy shelled manor 1675 and surrounding neighbourhood.	
	24.10.15	10.0am	Divine service for C.E. who are not on duty at Soyer Farm. C.O. goes to Armentieres to see trenches	N.D.K.
	24.10.15	10.30	Report received that C.O. hurt his stumbled in Armentieres and fallen on CO's leg breaking it above the ankle. Removed to 2nd Northumbrian Field Ambulance. Visited during day by Senior Major and M.O.	N.D.K.

2353 Wt. W2544/1454 700,000 5/15 D.D. & L. A.D.S.S./Forms/C. 2118.

Army Form C. 2118.

WAR DIARY
or
INTELLIGENCE SUMMARY.
(Erase heading not required.)

11th (S) Bn Cheshire Regt.

Place	Date	Hour	Summary of Events and Information	Remarks and references to Appendices
PLOEGSTEERT WOOD	25.10.15	ante	Nothing of importance to note during morning. In afternoon noticed at once that their wire had been put up by enemy in loop from left trench 113.	
		11 pm	Sentry observed bright light above parapet near BIRDCAGE 117 still from our own battery fire 9ft 119 at this hour.	
		10.30 pm	Enemy machine gun opened H.E. no flashes seen but sound indicates gun being fired from parapet near day H.Q. Also on 120 Enemy M.Gr swept BIRDCAGE.	
		11 pm	Phosphorus bombs dropped on our wire just short of parapet & formed for about 4 hour. Our artillery by request fired into enemy parapet (116) Nothing observed by our listening patrols. Enemy quiet. Bad weather evening with many flares to guide way. Rainy the whole day. Ordnance trench was of larrail from out. 4/5 their men worked in LE GHEER a little while (Verses 29) probably a spade could be seen working also a send 4gn windmill. Rounds deg answering talkings & group to EKS.W.B'S. Front quiet. Don't weight for some days. Night quiet.	N.D.K.
	26.10.15	3 pm	Artillery put 3 shells on enemy's wire off 113. From 7th to 4th armed force on to filled a comprehensive view of enemy trenches in conspicuous portions some sandbags of stuff material may indicate shortage of metal material. Work done on front of trenches in considerable. Windmill reported above now hidden. All work behind enemy wire. Cookhouses noticed & sandbag structures probably dug-outs. Possibly Germans constructing new barracks in front of the old bags.	
		3.30 pm	No of firer supports is large. No. of men & possibly these are Reserve troops. 2 H.E. shells dropped within our lines on at U.21.b.15.#.5 other U.21.b.2.2 no damage.	N.D.K.
		16.30 pm	One cap sent to B.H.E. (near 119 - 120)	N.D.K.
			Listening patrol reported sounds of work opposite; and 3 rounds were fired by D battery which stopped the noise having M.G. fire from U 22 C D.10	N.D.K.

2353 Wt.W2544/1454 700,000 5/15 D. D. & L. A.D.S.S./Forms/C. 2118.

Army Form C. 2118.

WAR DIARY
or
INTELLIGENCE SUMMARY.
(Erase heading not required.)

1st (S) Bn Cheshire Regt

Place	Date	Hour	Summary of Events and Information	Remarks and references to Appendices
PLOEGSTEERT WOOD	7/10/15	1 a.m.	Much sniping and converse heard in enemy's lines. Voices shouted "Peace is declared" (opp trench 113)	
		5 a.m.	White flag on stick placed about 60m in front of PICKET HOUSE. A dirty handkerchief may indicate men or trap concealed there. Sent to Bde. While dog very friendly & innocent looking 3 enemy snipers & night was very quiet, 1st to no sniping. Enemy periscopes hit by our snipers. The been to be learned from the past two days so little as possible should be informed in the early weather so that in wet weather by little as possible not be done, e.g. on ridge in a post should be seen at once at a slight distance behind the front line is also on left front telescope from a many periscopes.	
		11 a.m.	During the day a party of 2 officers and 65 men proceeded to Rwillent to a position held by Lt George's S.W.Bs relieved our men in the trenches. 6th S.W.Bs reported about 3' above parapet the machine gun section of men. A carpet (abgris?) party carrying planks which projected 115 of the C.T. most observed hurriedly from Walls to trench opposite. Daylight down men ununually quick. Scarcely attended by the enemy. Less sniping than on active, managed to hit at least one German from near & 3 pm. not a single shot was fired opposite two FT's and even 5 rounds rapid by two section between 6 & 7pm in T119 & T120 only elicited no very light. heard some firing in enemy's trench. They are undoubtedly relievers in T120 heard some second line in more comfortable for compass hug working. Possibly their second line is now heavy movement weather	
		6.30 pm 7 p.m.	Burst M.G. fires over Sunk Castle, NORWICH CASTLE Possibly enemy suspect " " parapet as par in PICKET HOUSE no working there.	
		10 p.m.	Three rifle grenades sent over by Germans, they short on over	

WAR DIARY
INTELLIGENCE SUMMARY

Army Form C. 2118.

1st (S) Batt. Cheshire Regt.

Place	Date	Hour	Summary of Events and Information	Remarks and references to Appendices
[illegible]	27/10/15	11 pm	Transport heard behind German lines in direction of HALTE in continuation of [illegible]	
ROAD			Le TOUQUET road	
			Trenches are in a very muddy state. The condition of the trenches behind the support lines of T.120, T.119, T.118, T.117 might be considerably bettered by raising both support lines and parapet about a foot, as in T.121. Weather — showery.	N.D.K.
			Weather grotting and parapet getting and parapet falled to work properly opposite T.116 and turnt into flinders on German flare failed to work. Buried with trench mortar light	
			Their own draws. Buried with trench mortar light for about a minute.	
			Germans again busy carrying planks into the F.T. for HALTE	
	28/10/15	4 pm	Part of our parapet fell in at T.117 also C.T. E parts was breaking down	
		10 am		
		4.20 pm 6.0 pm	A fire (perhaps a house afire) seen in [Warneton?] WARNETON. It was soon got under though it blazed bright for five minutes — out by 11.45 pm.	
		11.30 pm	One of the greatest needed, one of the greatest we had in the trenches. The hostilers were very quiet. Of course all day they may may account for inactivity. Only working party seen was the one carrying planks the Germans did no cuttings but seemed to be working in places by installing. The state of our wire. No artillery fire from the ending. Our men they night and day repairing trenches which are nothing very bullet.	
			It was in front of the trenches has been carefully examined by our patrols who found that it is not an good condition in places requires immediate attention. It is felt in front of T.112 and T.113 that we have not very good 114 — 111 has one for today mater [illegible] to wire 117 frontfile the patrol became [illegible] that a partly to wire 117 [illegible] with a wire of sang back not we [illegible]	W.D.K.
			T.115 — T.119 — T.120 more fire of possible [illegible] withdrew at [illegible] [illegible]	Top floor

Army Form C. 2118.

WAR DIARY
or
INTELLIGENCE SUMMARY.

(Erase heading not required.)

1st (S) Bn Cheshire Regt

Place	Date	Hour	Summary of Events and Information	Remarks and references to Appendices
PLOEGSTEERT WOOD	29/10/15	12 noon	Everything very quiet, no enemy seen and scarcely a shot fired. Enemy Artillery shelled T113 for a short time but did no damage beyond cutting the telephone wires for about 5 mins. Our own artillery inactive.	
	30/10/15		Relieved by the 8 S. Lancs during the afternoon. The men proceeded in an orderly manner and new quarters were taken up by us in Hdqrt farm in PLOEGSTEERT, when dangerous approaches being unavoidable & somewhat dangerous, owing to spent bullets. D Coy took up new billets. Aeroplanes were up early and were shelled with fairly quiet on the whole. Rats in the day being unusually quiet. An unusual amount of ? cases. Our own Artillery was fairly busy the whole day, an unusually few German shells coming over.	H.D.K.
	31/10/15		This day was fairly quiet, the second Artillery ration being fired off. One man was hit on the foot by a spent bullet near TOURVET BERTHE. Lt. Col. SIR H. LENNARD BT. assumed command of the Battalion which was Col ASPINALL'S unfortunate accident has been commended by Major FRENCH.	H.D.K.
	1/11/15		Nothing of importance occurred. The sniping increased during the day and a few enemy shells arrived in our trenches. They were effectively replied to. The weather excellent and the winter officers quarters at HANTS FM suffered in consequence.	H.D.K.

WRAD am Major
Commanding
11th Cheshire Regt

25th Hussars } 11th Ulster's Rgt. Vol. #2

121/7656

Nov 15. & Secbr

S. O.
13 sheets

Mr Cheshire
Vol: 3

121/7910

25th/5/iii

Army Form C. 2118.

WAR DIARY
or
INTELLIGENCE SUMMARY.
(Erase heading not required.)

Instructions regarding War Diaries and Intelligence Summaries are contained in F. S. Regs., Part II. and the Staff Manual respectively. Title pages will be prepared in manuscript.

Place	Date	Hour	Summary of Events and Information	Remarks and references to Appendices
HANTS FM	1/10/15		Nothing of importance occurred. Some what intense during the day and a few enemy shells arrived in our trenches. They were effectively replied to. The weather favourable to the minor operations HANTS FM suffered no annoyance.	N.A.K.
	2/10/15		Another uneventful day. Rain practically continuous. Fatigue parties working on R.E.	
	3/10/15		During the morning there were a few moments of shelling to both sides using up yesterday's rations. PLOEGSTEERT was said to have been shelled. Our artillery also was busy. Afternoon & evening quiet. During the day two new machine guns were prepared for the entry of the S. Lancs.	
	4/10/15		The morning was quiet except for doubtful shelling and three aeroplanes seen. In mid-afternoon the new trench mortars was ready to fire. Rainy but not Rainy but the prisoners and our battalion took over the trenches during the day.	
PLOEGSTEERT WOOD			State of trenches – When taken over the trenches had suffered severely owing to the recent wet weather. Trench 120 was under water but portable 119 completely under water. 118 very bad. In places 117 was very bad and the parapets 116 114 very bad 115 difficult. 116 was lying in a few places from 24 yards back 110 was the last of the line to suffer for though the trenches but the trenches like they are only made possible by trying the shoulder to ground but by the traverses but the flank the apparently to protect the parapets on trench on which a draft treatments only with partially possible. In parts there are on trenches being raised. The flooring was affected by rain, the improvements made to a drainage it as begun.	A.D.S.S./Forms/C.2118.

Army Form C. 2118.

WAR DIARY
or
INTELLIGENCE SUMMARY.

(Erase heading not required.)

Instructions regarding War Diaries and Intelligence Summaries are contained in F. S. Regs., Part II. and the Staff Manual respectively. Title pages will be prepared in manuscript.

Place	Date	Hour	Summary of Events and Information	Remarks and references to Appendices
PLOEGSTEERT WOOD	4/11/15		It seems a great oversight that the Division occupied this section last winter did not leave any suggestions as to drainage. The works immediately in front of the Hampshires were almost impassable. The only with digging was the Rue Ligere Road and Norfolk Avenue.	A.D.
	5/11/15	7pm	Everything quiet in and in front of T. 119. Fire opened on enemy working party opposite 120. Enemy quiet and had enemy working on their parapet opposite 120. Wire	
		4am	S/Lt Riley went out to centre of T.119 in thin condition in front of which a fair shot of our trench is covered by an observation of 121 & 122	
		2am 4am	this trench fell short of our trench. Very lights used by enemy. In fact our trench on which we rely most for defence. B.11 dift 3 sets of halliards were unfortunately unserviceable water work tied up for 3 holidays. Was unsafe. Last enemy to trench.	
			Enemy machine from location 117 (U22 C 3½.9) that has been located opposite T. 111	
			Enemy patrols not seen as usual, something heard along F.T. opposite T. 111	
		10am	Shells which all morning on the FIRM ACRE, two shell by high field were by a german battery that stood enemy fire the 11/15. Our field artillery fire	
		6pm	transport on the right of our sector followed by night artillery. Bannew	
			went up to T. 119 at trying to take the "I want to go home" we night. Bannew was kept in at trench and however the parapet from 113 to 117 though we did not fire on	
		10pm	A machine gun trained on our hurst german parapet. Our own trouble was in parts. Without falter, can hurt german hearts at lately and before even overhead as it were by to keep the 11 S.L.s out except at T. 111	
			Fire then they were to say something PATROL have was no trouble was the	
			parts of D coy on front. S/Lt S.L. Anglo lines was by us nearly safe. Hampshire House was relieved by Hampshire nearly very big to Peche Villa were a post chief	
			and water for several hours and arrangements in being placed	

Army Form C. 2118.

WAR DIARY
or
INTELLIGENCE SUMMARY.
(Erase heading not required.)

Instructions regarding War Diaries and Intelligence Summaries are contained in F. S. Regs., Part II. and the Staff Manual respectively. Title pages will be prepared in manuscript.

Place	Date	Hour	Summary of Events and Information	Remarks and references to Appendices
PLOEGSTEERT WOOD	6/11/15	6-9am	A few shots fired from BIRDCAGE E. Four rifle grenades were thrown into the BIRDCAGE shortly afterwards. Our working parties were steadily out & the plank was carried along 119 + 120 and inside trench, sounds of mallets were heard. Enemy and my section while they mostly Germans spent themselves for a short time, one man over the parapet. Enemy artillery was quiet during the day.	
		9-12 noon	Work proceeded on our side chiefly throughout the day went on a dry but frequent on the trenches and the parapet which need to be drawn & powdered mullion especially along the communication trench, was carried on being myself rebuilt & trying there in many places. Work was carried on especially about which was cold and nasty. The day was fair & even falling but Myself	
		8pm	Rifle grenades thrown at position T118 + 119. I short, other over. 2 others were also from tanks near trench 121. Enemy rifle fire broke on the enemy near trench 121. Enemy rifle fire broke out also westward thrown in T115 –116 and enemy M.G. opened fire, probably by one of three but could from T115. Saw heads of enemy when our work patrol in the light of flares but could	
	10p		The right covering our line at our signal sent up parties not discernible. The head of C.T. SAP 117, on T supporting party	
	10.10pm		They were passed over T from LEAGER Rd & the	
	10.30pm		fly went scatter very quietly had 6 scatter very quietly came over parapet T. 1116 117 all burnt very sunny prompt out down (over BIRDCAGE) Enemy's fire ceased 1105 rifle fire from 120 but not ground and went cowed from	
	10.55		made observer cleft occult lay took and patrol from 120 but not ground and went cowed from	
			??? lay took and patrol from BIRDCAGE) Enemy 6 or 24 hours fuel so worth if the whole of the trench is great interest and rests ??? left. A support but 3 day with were very conflict with the completion of them and with the enemy may work it, we may and also at his very right one can conclude them range, bury and wit they had were two long of one conducting way in my sights. Missing from the rain it will not any shots be of men working ??? to pay ??? be far.	

2353 Wt. W354/1454 700,000 5/15 D.D. & L. A.D.S.S./Forbis/C. 2118.

WAR DIARY
or
INTELLIGENCE SUMMARY.
(Erase heading not required.)

Army Form C. 2118.

Instructions regarding War Diaries and Intelligence Summaries are contained in F.S. Regs., Part II. and the Staff Manual respectively. Title pages will be prepared in manuscript.

Place	Date	Hour	Summary of Events and Information	Remarks and references to Appendices
PLOEGSTEERT WOOD	8/11/15	5.15 a.m.	Sgt Major Russell bagged a German. The latter was seen to fall backward into his trench.	
		6.30 a.m.	Another (120) French - German soldier on parapet driving stakes in with large mallet. He was brought down by one of our men. His loophole has been contracted opposite 116.	
		11 a.m.	Our artillery fired at a MG emplacement off 112 but did not get a direct hit. Several whizz-bangs and 4 Rifle grenades came from 120.	
		7.30 p.m.	Have run french by Germans towards their own support lines. These were replied to by light signals jumbled back. Some melted. Perhaps of signalling for transport. Light signals observed in N' left attached again of nothing lit. Green lights seen from behind ♦ the BIRDCAGE	
		11 p.m.	Enemy very light active but MG fire occasionally. Plank nearly along trench 1/18. OHD 115 steam again. Enemy appeared more intent on working trenches. Sniping not very good work.	
	9/11/15	8 a.m.	Our artillery and infantry doing their + caused considerable retaliation. HE whizz bangs but little coming from the enemy big M with a number of working parties and we were very lucky to have 3 casualties. There shells fell in front of HUNTERS AVENUE and about C.T. 115. Our morning work is proceeding in the trenches. The company worked hard at drainage & on parapet. Exceptionally good work has been done by the right company. B Coy on HAMPSHIRE LANE and "B" Coy working work offhand of water and I started that the ditches ran [illegible] from ST 117 past RIFLE HOUSE to ESSEX FARM & so on towards PLOEG ♦ STEERT and soon to check by the R.E. the fact that there existed the trenches which formed not by an important part at present very defective.	

KB 2353 Wt. W2544/1454   700,000   5/15   D.D. & L.   A.D.S.S./Forms/C. 2118.

Army Form C. 2118.

WAR DIARY
or
INTELLIGENCE SUMMARY.
(Erase heading not required.)

Place	Date	Hour	Summary of Events and Information	Remarks and references to Appendices
PLOEGSTEERT WOOD	9/11/15	6 a.m.	A few rounds fired from BIRDCAGE at 119-120 enemy lines off 117 length I immediately went out & Hancock went out on patrol from 180 & found that some was thought in, that cupple was presently without much apart the supporting officers and cupple it.	
	9/11/15	9.30 p.m.		
	10/11/15	6 a.m.	A German work outside their parapet was discovered opposite PIG/JET HOUSE A red & yellow & black flag was being placed on the our M.G. ground fire while flag was being placed near the flag, warning soldiers caps, but the photograph, could be seen. After five from M.G.s they replied with 3 rifle grenades which fell behind our lines. From window of T 11/2 & 113 the trouble r/f/e (our boy with MG. practically P & T 11/4, 115 houses was a very quiet - in bits were a regularly up the letters, and Barry bury at work flags seen in bits enough to render sufficient no 91 would continuing from 6.30 p.m. he were in 113 to 114s, one morning a witness Consequently Brightest operations in 113 to 716 were in Brigades smelt pumps I water transport were in parapet flowed over from (cause effected by Empl between T water let to two apparently different now 1 course effected that all tracks were rather than yesterday but 113, 114, 115 & 116 no so much yet not T 117 & T & T & 115 is very had & No 115 where you period is sadly restricting 119, 120 water much had except near German house (GERMAN HOUSE)	
			HUNTERS AVENUE quite good such freshness nat. in repairs & rebuilding continues & dugouts, the engineers & Ryle took over the drainage came out. I made day apparatus effect I clear the ditches where water is flowing away from the trenches I had seen the trenches going to help the drainage of the infantry should I had into the water & trenches at of the water where to flowly emptied by these totalling have an efficient & (efficient calm). To bear pumping made a few cut by storm which flows readily T 117 118 119 canvid (be sheared & some extent by storm which flows readily)	

Army Form C. 2118.

WAR DIARY
or
INTELLIGENCE SUMMARY.
(Erase heading not required.)

Place	Date	Hour	Summary of Events and Information	Remarks and references to Appendices
Ploegsteert Wood	10.11.15		LONDON BRIDGE and what is left cloyed up with weeds Candelabra & other parts was actually got together to clear there grown but it was put into the effect hand of the engineers who seen to have most neat idea - than they can do to be the cheapest form of trench support which the limiters as timber framework, at an short intervals between the family trench as timber framework. It should be possible to start them as well as to communication trenches. Another thing which should be considered on is the fact that of buildings are built at 60 feet an outward slope they will & often slide away of the bottom and the whole hayput fall into trench. This may be avoided (a) by careful pegging & not cutting into profile (b) by choosing a firm foundation & finishing the courses / sandbags [sketch drawn] note Building falled with broken bricks seem to weather best	
		2 p.m.	The Battalion was relieved by R. D'Batt. Surt Lancashire Reg. The 11.D.C.L.I was complete by 4 pm. HEADQUARTERS took over used billets in Game Keepers Cottages situated on S.W. corner of PLOEGSTEERT WOOD. Companies took over former billets.	
	11.11.15		Ordinary Day and routine, enemy artillery activity on back area where heard	
	12.11.15		PLOEGSTEERT was again shelled - One shell dropped in a cellar, others were hidden still very bad	
	13.11.15		Misty day. Enemy Dropped some H.E. Shells around PLOEGSTEERT passed 5.45pm	
	14.11.15	3.15pm	A clear bright day. We came front at M/11L Artillery active on both sides - Enemy shelled NEUVE EGLISE leaving a certain amount of ...	
		4.30pm	Burst of enemy artillery shells dropped in and around PLOEGSTEERT MAROCCON MULLER - Burst of machine gun shells during the day between 11.00 - 11.30pm	
		3 pm	Enemy dropped about forty shells into NEUVE EGLISE	

Army Form C. 2118.

WAR DIARY
INTELLIGENCE SUMMARY.
(Erase heading not required.)

Instructions regarding War Diaries and Intelligence Summaries are contained in F. S. Regs., Part II. and the Staff Manual respectively. Title pages will be prepared in manuscript.

Place	Date	Hour	Summary of Events and Information	Remarks and references to Appendices
Ploegsteert Wood	15.XI.15		Weather fair & frosty. Enemy snipers fire shots on road between Touquet Berthe and Ploegsteert. Enemy also fired several salvos of H.E. into Neuve Eglise at about 3.30 p.m. Otherwise quiet day.	Cpt 1
	16.XI.15		Hostile artillery quiet. Artillery activity of our Batteries away. K gives back his way.	Cpt 1
T.113 – 120 (reserve)		2 A.M.	The Battalion returned to B Coy Batt, Scots Guards billets at 2 p.m. Relief completed without incident. On our right flank the 3rd Batt. Border Regt was relieved by the 2nd Batt. Scots Fusiliers the relief was completed. This Section on our left was relieved by the 1st Wiltshire Regt and Dorsetshire Regt. Enemy snipers were active & often sniping were heard in enemy's lines - spent 2 s. No firing was heard.	
	17.XI.15		Enemy front was rather quiet shortly before attack. It being rather misty. No firing and no sniping heard.	Cpt 1
		3.30 A.M.	Enemy observed some men entering through the trench opposite T.114 (Picket House). Enemy was observed strengthening N about H.006 - Red Feb. green fire flare was exposed - No other developments along enemy lines. Too few men were observed on the line. An increased number of flares were noted in enemy trenches and his rifle guns were Seen 2 at larger pits ranges.	
		4.30 A.M.	Sentry on listening post in front of Picket House observed two to three enemy approached & halted 25 yards from wire. No relief. They were seen short serves Cape.	Cpt 1
		9.50 P.M.	One Machine Gun suspected the enemy is about 300 yards speech T.113	
	18.XI.15	12.30 A.M.	The enemy observation balloon was seen today. Seen S.W. Warneton Church and K a trip in the direction of Messines.	
			Our own officers patrols were twice fired on by low R.t. Machine gun fire from the target but attacked as a result. No attempt returned the fire. K enemy's line sniped - West furthered repeated without firing the day.	Cpt 1
	19.XI.15	2.30 A.M.	Capt Dunn examined G ground in front of Picket House in order to get hints & sketch. Two N.C.O's he found that the Allemand called out "H le Gheer Road" round with loud a journal glacis. The place is now safe & enemy's trenches.	
		3 A.M.	Capt Dunn returned & noted no 15 yards the enemy lined, heard a German answer. A sentry was dispatched into trench - it seems that S. Le Gheer Road descended sounding the party + K Ensenot & half hour before dawn. These men were empty handed, going to I.K. German Country purposely in an attempt to hear to today's Ensenot's line of lewdly time, to provide a force & lied up a heavy blankets field. In good condition to get luck/hoar. The troop line to present was party of companies with plenty. Enemy snipers appeared to be from 15 to 20 yards apart.	Cpt 1

WAR DIARY
INTELLIGENCE SUMMARY

Army Form C. 2118.

Place	Date	Hour	Summary of Events and Information	Remarks and references to Appendices
Ploegsteert Wood. T.113.120 (inclusive)	19 Aug	5.10 am	Enemy sent up a red rocket opposite PICKET HOUSE - The number of German infantry manning the trenches opposite LE GHEER appear much increased and apparently hold the - One working party in NORFOLK AVENUE not much interfered with by our fire. Our Snipers report the enemy has been rather inactive in the area opposite LE GHEER and LES PELERINS, his snipers may be sniping as usual in these areas, though it appears they periodically fire at the places passing to & fro. They practically took up the chorus of victory apparently being sustained there somewhere in these neighbourhoods. There has been most unusual amount of rifle fire on both sides during the period. Enemy has been sending parties with new and fresh munitions.	EE
		1 pm	An Enemy Aeroplane flying S.W. was seen 5 B 9/3 a fair height. A small splinter of the Enemy Shrapnel 4.7 on 5"Shrapnel shell fell near support trench 118. A few shells dropping in the vicinity of chemical works & tramway.	
		4.30 pm	An enemy aeroplane was seen 5 B 9/3 & R11 Pict Parc opened with H.E. & Shr. shells white smoke. No significance of appreciable effect shells opened up near R11 & R15.	
		10.5 pm	A party was seen 7.11.5 near the enemy's lines opposite T115. Westward towards PLOEGSTEERT Approach 11 pm. Enemy continued mortar bomb on the trenches and his rifle fire has been noticeably more heavier than.	
	20 Aug	11.30 am	An enemy shell struck a tree about 30 yds in front of T117 Germans started.	
		12 m	One shell fired a stretcher from 20 yards of Front T117. Considerable damage was done to our own parapet.	EE
		2 pm	An enemy working party was seen taking material for & communication trench S of R.15 LE GHEER HALTE ROAD. Some were treated in dark blue and seen in grey.	
		6 pm	An enemy working party near the right terminal the BIRDCAGE was watched by our artillery	
		9.3 pm	An enemy working party of about 30 men seen going to right working party No T.11, came up Battery S to Parapet Enemy rifles were slack & Veil.

Army Form C. 2118.

WAR DIARY
~~INTELLIGENCE SUMMARY.~~
(Erase heading not required.)

Instructions regarding War Diaries and Intelligence Summaries are contained in F. S. Regs., Part II. and the Staff Manual respectively. Title pages will be prepared in manuscript.

Place	Date	Hour	Summary of Events and Information	Remarks and references to Appendices
PLOEGSTEERT Wood	21.11.15	9.30am	Our artillery fired which rounds into the trench which was marked the Birdcage. Good practice was made. It is supposed that this turned to a machine gun employed against our aeroplanes which we had noticed mainly active.	App
		4 pm	Five pigeons seen flying from the direction of WARNETON over PLOEGSTEERT WOOD. They appeared to come from our PIGEON HOUSE enemy post and seen carrying baskets from them which hindered them taking aerial photography to drop.	
	22.11.15		A quiet morning. The Battalion was relieved by the 2nd Bn. South Lancashire Regt. The relief was completed by 4 pm. The 5th Border Regt. on the right were also relieved by the 2nd Bn. South Lancashire Regt. The Battalion occupied the former billets. B and C Companies in huts on the road - A Company at TOUQUET BERTHE FARM 3rd Company in PLOEGSTEERT and Headquarters at CRESLOW.	App
Subsidiary line Locality "J"	23.11.15		A quiet day during. PLOEGSTEERT received the usual number of shells but no damage was done. Artillery on both sides fired considerably throughout the day.	App
	24.11.15		Weather much in each morning but lifting at about 9 am an artillery duel ensued. Enemy fire about forty shells in and around PLOEGSTEERT and also shelled other points probably in search of our batteries. In the afternoon enemy gun batteries kept up a continuous bombardment until dusk. The enemy reply was slight.	App
	25.11.15		Incessant artillery activity on the part of enemy. Fourteen shells fell in & near our HQ at Locality "J" and forty near our headquarters. A quiet day near our lines.	App

Army Form C. 2118.

WAR DIARY
INTELLIGENCE SUMMARY.
(Erase heading not required.)

Instructions regarding War Diaries and Intelligence Summaries are contained in F. S. Regs., Part II. and the Staff Manual respectively. Title pages will be prepared in manuscript.

Place	Date	Hour	Summary of Events and Information	Remarks and references to Appendices
Ploegsteert Wood	26.9.15		Weather fine. Good frost. Usual artillery fire on both sides & aircraft activity.	—
Erquinghem Lys	27.9.15		The Battalion relieved the 8th Batt South Lancashire Regt in Trenches 113 – 123 inclusive. The relief of our company was carried out in the Evening owing to shelling all day. The relief was completed by 9 p.m. without any unusual incidents occurring. On our left flank are the 1st Batt Wiltshires & on our right flank the 2nd Batt South Lancashire Regt. The night passed quietly. Bright moonlight after 10 p.m.	—
T 113–120	28 Sept. 3 a.m.		Some Enemy shells passed over PLOEGSTEERT WOOD in the direction of MAISON 1875. There was lively bombardment of an IC (Enemy) Communication trench — Enemy destroyed the earthwork behind their trench at LE GHEER-HALTE ROAD. It is suspected that a new trench is being dug behind his old trench. Enemy was kept on alert. His machine was observed flying in a hostile direction all day and reported flying low over TOUQUET BERTHE at 5-30 p.m. Suddenly something [?] her own batteries and at 9 p.m. the hostile aeroplanes were observed. They dropped three white lights which burst knee-high & starts were thrown up a rocket which TUP at 7-30 p.m. The enemy searchlight is at present unknown. Our artillery fired nine rounds & also opened the machine gun BIRDCAGE. Our [illegible] ...	E.G.

WAR DIARY
INTELLIGENCE SUMMARY
(Erase heading not required.)

Army Form C. 2118.

Place	Date	Hour	Summary of Events and Information	Remarks and references to Appendices
Ploegsteert WOOD	29.xi.15		A quiet day. The enemy burst shrapnel over Essex Farm in the direction of T.112 & 113. A shell was left over MH rifle grenade was put over Bomb (605). The Enemy continuing to carry water down his communication trenches towards his front attack — We were concentrating of a shoot supported by the Brigade A.C. The shrapnel was observed over T. BIRDCAGE — living parties were seen in front of T.112.	C31
T.115–120 (inclusive)	30.xi.15		Enemy more active than usual. In reply to our trench mortars registering on T. BIRDCAGE the enemy trench Ex.P.J. Wd.J.bays ct. and around T.120 — both MG Trenches & new salients being rapidly constructed and also large Mes being lobbed onto the parados. He emerged most aggressively the enemy also dropped 12 shells into Ft. Rifleman trench & LEGWEAR —	
		12.45p.	Lieut. Ford, Machine Gun Officer, Batt. observing at PICKET HOUSE, was severely wounded in the head by an enemy sniper, the first shots in fact fired. Successive shots came thru a loop hole in the wall. He was carried under apparent fire to BAILLEUL hospital but unfortunately succumbed to his wounds during the night. On working parties reported but shelling of the night in front of T.113 M.38 W.115 & 119 —	C31
	1.xii.15		Our artillery made a demonstration during the day. This consisted of the shelling of FACTORY FARM for one hour, shelling Enemy's front N. of T. BIRDCAGE for one hour, and shelling Enemy's front & communication trenches N. of T. BIRDCAGE for half an hour. Good results were noted. The enemy front & communication trenches N. of T. BIRDCAGE were fully occupied at the time. The enemy's front system was hit fairly often but never returned to pre-war state & was silent.	C31

(Continued) D.D.&L.

Army Form C. 2118.

WAR DIARY
INTELLIGENCE SUMMARY
(Erase heading not required.)

11th (S) Batt. Cheshire Regt.

Place	Date	Hour	Summary of Events and Information	Remarks and references to Appendices
Maple Redt Wood Pts 118-120 (inclusive)	Jan 1st		Howitzers 118-120 As well as shelling the Wood heavier both 10% and 4.5 Howitzers were causing heavy casualties - There was the usual support of trench mortars & rifle grenade bombardments. Capt Spear and Lieut Keeling killed by trench mortar fire. Total casualties 10 NCOs & men killed 15 - B - One Sentry N.C.O. perished from exposure 16 - A - Of the five obtained in BIRDCAGE none appear to have sense [illegible] but none as yet. Shews the present our boundary post by rifle fire. one of the enemy trenches and two machine guns played on Battalion the night two mortars were also frequently used. The enemy's parapet dist 15 has been swept by fire nearly away night. B. coy's No. working party was dispersed just N of a. BIRDCAGE The Battalion was relieved during the day by the 8th Batt South Lancashire Regt. One Company was relieved after dark and the remainder on 2 pm.	
	2nd		A company reached Quiet day.	appx 1
CRESSON	3rd		Weather hot and very unsettled. The day was very quiet. A few rounds 9'' were fired by the artillery in each side. Gases slowly. Battalion unsettled.	appx 1
	4th		The [illegible] relieved the Wood in the S. by D Battalion. Enemy dropped a few shells into NEUSTADT Headquarters and to be fine our artillery fired 10 rounds front wearly dropping [illegible] [illegible] the trenches. The enemy except perhaps for a large [illegible] this day.	appx 1

Army Form C. 2118.

WAR DIARY
or
INTELLIGENCE SUMMARY
(Erase heading not required.)

11th (S) Batt. Cheshire Regt.

Place	Date	Hour	Summary of Events and Information	Remarks and references to Appendices
PLOEGSTEERT	5.11.15		A bright day after a wet & stormy night. At about 2 or 3 pm enemy dropped two "whistles" just behind PLOEGSTEERT. At about 3 pm our Battery commenced shelling our own lines and killed by one of our own munitions. The enemy's trenches were hit as a/c of Bty were drawing hits on a chine from fire in Machine shell factory. Enemy's attitude quiet. No Bty of any importance. Our Bnkr (Bertin) visited our position & Col. Hall of 1.16.15. Bn Command. Tr Battalion - Tr Battalion retired & Tr Plot Battn Comde heads to T.18-20 (inclusive) during the day. The weather was unsettled during day & frequent artillery practice was made by several places - a lot of rumours. A bombard after mid [...] 12 HAMPSHIRE Tr. Mk. III [...] trench mortar went blasted enemy Mortar, firing excellent specimens [...] for cause, Buntings Alt trench break with a 5 sniper D - first shot of company opposite T.117-118.-	Ref
	6.11.15			
	7.11.15			
,, ,, (Nieppe)	8.11.15		Misty, Foggy with Showers. About 5.30 am, an enemy biplane flying towards TU3 was caught & fired by our anti-aircraft guns and Driven off by machine gun fire. At 11.30am another PLOEGSTEERT. Aeroplane was flying in the direction of MESSINES and driven by anti aircraft gun over our lines. An enemy biplane with the by our S.I. Bfd in the evening in 1E direction of NIEPPE. At 3.30 pm a Taub was seen an old [...] flying in the [...] Enemy dropped bombs making a low aerial to a MaIK Tug [...]	

Army Form C. 2118.

WAR DIARY
or
INTELLIGENCE SUMMARY
(Erase heading not required.)

11th (S) Batt. Cheshire Regt.

Place	Date	Hour	Summary of Events and Information	Remarks and references to Appendices
FOREST GATE WOOD TA3-120 (Picturne)	8 [month]		It proved in front of the BIRDCAGE - The road was found to be very promiscuously shell-pitted with hip-long craters. No place of ponto- of covered approach. A working party was taken up to this [?] DEEP DUGOUT from HQ by F.18 at 7 p.m. ... [illegible handwritten continuation]	
"	"	4 p.m.	[illegible handwritten continuation]	

Army Form C. 2118.

WAR DIARY
or
INTELLIGENCE SUMMARY.
(Erase heading not required.)

11th (S) Batt. Cheshire Regt.

G3/1

Place	Date	Hour	Summary of Events and Information	Remarks and references to Appendices
PLOEGSTEERT WOOD Tus-120 (inclusive)	9.11.15		Our own artillery dropped seven [...] shells outside the parapet of Tr No. 117. Damaging our [...]. Several shells burst near Company Headquarters Tr No. [...] one passed through the parapet of Tr No. Unsqueteen. 12 shells came into [...] parapet in and around our trenches 118-119. Opposite Tr No. 119 enemy's [...] appeared. A rifle was fired and the [...] fired [...] in reference always the [...]. 6 shots should be [...] to [...]. Enemy fired a [...] to [...] Tr No. Shells were being [...] [...] [...] [...]. At 12 am an enemy machine gun [...] opened [...] [...] to [...] our [...]. 2 am MG [...] [...] [...] [...] [...] [...] heavier [...] [...].	
	10.11.15	12.30am (m?)	Another SOS had been sent [...] [...] [...]. [...] [...] [...] [...] 7.20. They returned at [...] CT. Ballonire. A patrol in Sgt Hone [...] [...] to [...] SYEGERHOUSE in the [...] point 15 yards N of R cluster [...] IR BIRDCAGE. They returned [...] [...] having [...] [...]. [...] they [...] returned to [...] SWG power [...] [...] [...] [...] of this front [...] [...] [...] [...] [...] [...] [...] [...] 3 deep. [...] [...] [...] [...] [...] [...] IR BIRDCAGE to a point 15 yards N of C point 10 yards N of R cluster [...] IR BIRDCAGE [...] [...] from LA TRUIE to GERMAN HOUSE in [...] [...] [...] [...] [...].	

Army Form C. 2118.

WAR DIARY
OF
INTELLIGENCE SUMMARY.
(Erase heading not required.)

11th (S) Batt. Cheshire Regt.

Place	Date	Hour	Summary of Events and Information	Remarks and references to Appendices
PLOEGSTEERT WOOD T113.120 (extension)	March 5	6 pm	Signal rifle grenades were sent over by the enemy dropping behind T119 0.30 which set the object of exposing our party working on T15 new trench.	
		9.30	The men of A Coys on Coy and B Coys GERMAN HUTS. On y these struck a man who was not at present wounded. During the day several dummy bombers hoists were treated and fired on by our snipers.	
			25 H.E. enemy shells burst over our support trench in the wood.	
	March 13	6	Showers. Several enemy shells were sent over the night of T.20 between 4-5 pm.	
		5 pm		
		M.M	6 bombing patrol returned from R119 T.UD. The dits manned F.S. y PIROCAGE. Contained about 40 y shells + T.L. battery front at the end. It was unoccupied. It was occupied to hold it has had in the evening there a few may perced that seen several escapes of enemy hotile. No sign of a working party towards opening the way here & frequent use busied on S. HALTE - PONT ROUGE ROAD since y Halte. The billets arranged against y T24 could for an enemy stand light and less burning the fourth company whole of shea front	
	March 5	9 am	Our Lewis Machine Guns were any lines lifting to 10 trenches of Warneton. holding two prisoners being a man smoker. bringing our lines. Work had commenced on T15 new trench yet no report...	

WAR DIARY / INTELLIGENCE SUMMARY

Army Form C. 2118.

11th (S) Batt. Cheshire Regt.

Place	Date	Hour	Summary of Events and Information	Remarks and references to Appendices
PLUGSTREET WOOD T.43.120 (afterwards) CRESLOW (huts in Hutbourne)	12 & 13		The Battalion took over trenches T.113-120 (inclusive) from 8 S. Batt Scott. Lancashire Rgt in two reliefs. The Company relief commenced at 10 a.m. and was completed at 2 p.m.	
	14.11.15		Inspection of Batt. billets etc on 14/11/15 at 11 a.m. Nothing of note cleared.	
T.113-120 (Hutbourne)	15/11/15		The Battalion took over trenches T113-120 (inclusive) from 8 S. Batt S. Lancs relief less during the day. Relief commenced & completed at 3.15 p.m. Snipers of enemy active from trench. Rainy & wet. 3 men wounded from one shot. Enemy opened rapid machine gun & rifle fire at 6.15 about 5 am. The morning of the 18th. Patrols working between lines at night (both sides) found enemy's wire much damaged by our patrols ... trenches of the enemy were ... 3 wounded others to be trusted much of the trench. The rest of the day patrols were quiet (no firing), mostly at work of drainage & a few machine guns fired at night on the lines of communication.	
	18 a.m.		Night patrol sent out accompanied patrol a bomb party attempts to bomb... Battery School training mines Head Quarters night to Snipers use being one ... night Rear Bays T.123 Dug out. 31 casualties ... than been pre... on ...	

Army Form C. 2118.

WAR DIARY
or
INTELLIGENCE SUMMARY.
(Erase heading not required.)

11th (S) Batt. Cheshire Regt.

Instructions regarding War Diaries and Intelligence Summaries are contained in F. S. Regs., Part II. and the Staff Manual respectively. Title pages will be prepared in manuscript.

Place	Date	Hour	Summary of Events and Information	Remarks and references to Appendices
HURSTERT WOOD TH3-120 (inclusive)	April 15		A relatively quiet day. Our sytem to patrol in front that we adhered to as our men found nothing live of [illegible] enemy M.G. post from the BIRDCAGE.	
			Without success. Our heavy machine guns were located at the BIRDCAGE.	
			The following activity was observed during last 48 hours. 15 days -	
		9.30	Biplane flew over our lines towards E.	
		10.30	Pigeon seen flying from S.E. of MESSINES.	
		11.50	do do do	
		11.55	do do do	
		12.50	Biplane seen flying in the direction of WARNETON at a high altitude.	
		12.55	do do do	
			During the day the sound of heavy firing was heard in the BIRDCAGE by one of our battle patrols. At the same time enemy working party [illegible]	
		2.30	The 58th French Mortar Battery fired 4 rounds [illegible]	
			[illegible]	
			Enemy artillery reported very active. Reports being received of [illegible]	
			harassing activity enemy trenches.	
			A heavy storm (and showers) fell in the F.G. & N and east of MESSINES and S.	
	April 16		A quiet day with the exception of some enemy activity on our [illegible]	
			[illegible]	

Army Form C. 2118.

WAR DIARY
or
INTELLIGENCE SUMMARY.
(Erase heading not required.)

11th (S) Batt. Cheshire Regt.

Instructions regarding War Diaries and Intelligence Summaries are contained in F. S. Regs., Part II. and the Staff Manual respectively. Title pages will be prepared in manuscript.

Place	Date	Hour	Summary of Events and Information	Remarks and references to Appendices
PICK[ETHOUSE] area	20.11.15		[illegible] trenches — near ST.119 & 118 & ST.117, between PALK VILLA, northeast PICKETHOUSE, in LE GHEER village. (There are trench communications) [illegible] depth of trench exposed in parts — [illegible] [illegible] was serviced against overhangers —	App
	21st		[illegible] and mostly accurate. [illegible] [illegible] [illegible] [illegible] [illegible] several casualties occurred. [illegible] were reported & [illegible]	
		12 noon	7 [illegible] [illegible] just near GERMAN HOUSE. Trench [illegible] [illegible] [illegible] [illegible] [illegible] [illegible] & [illegible].	
			On [illegible] [illegible] [illegible] [illegible] [illegible] heavy [illegible] [illegible] [illegible] fire.	
		11 a.m.	3 whizzbangs fell on [illegible] ST.TM3, killed [illegible] [illegible] [illegible] [illegible] [illegible]	
		6.9 pm	[illegible] trench [illegible] on trench. Enemy's addition fire [illegible] heavier —	
	22nd		[illegible] [illegible] [illegible] [illegible] from 11. Lt.? Th6 of [illegible] R.F.A.? relieved 115 S. [illegible] BIRDCAGE [illegible] in arrival of the patrol on 11. with [illegible] post, 3 [illegible] at Hq which fired on 11. Party [illegible] BIRDCAGE close by. — Lieut. [illegible] came round to [illegible] he found it — [illegible] [illegible] [illegible] — at 8.45 pm his Party was [illegible] in Cy near M.R.	App
	23 [illegible] 12 hrs		On [illegible] [illegible] [illegible] party was supposed [illegible] in 4 pts. [illegible] 2 in EGG PIE FORT in [illegible] season & officer's mess [illegible] the [illegible] [illegible] [illegible] during the day by 11/ Brigade. [illegible] [illegible] [illegible]	App

2353 Wt. W2544/1454 700,000 5/15 D. D. & L. A.D.S.S./Forms/C. 2118.

Army Form C. 2118.

WAR DIARY
or
INTELLIGENCE SUMMARY.
(Erase heading not required.)

11th Batt. Cheshire Regt.

Place	Date	Hour	Summary of Events and Information	Remarks and references to Appendices
PLOEGSTEERT WOOD (RESERVE) (Huts)	25th May 1916		Military preparations resumed. Heavy artillery fire on both sides.	Ett
	26th		The Battalion relieved the 2nd Battalion South Lancashire Regt. in Trenches 113-120 (inclusive) at 5.30 am.	Ett
T113-120 (inclusive)	28th May 5.4 pm	2.30 pm	Our infantry, trench mortars bombarded the BIRDCAGE but suspected - Enemy retaliated on T130, behind our lines our trench mortars, our supports, and also searched the front for our guns. The trench mortars were heard to fire off six rounds, found to be trained away to the employment's supposing in the Infr. mainly found. Trenches from that reported hearing hopping noises M.G. Emplacements in T118 - Enemy guns were occasionally active, but Infr. supposed Enemy counting was not opened. Enemy Snipers were active during the night. On fire Enemy shelling her escape. The heavy Thor. includes - Their enemy's infantry practice of power from her Support line disposed of by rifle fire. Opposite T118 at 9.15 pm, a trench explosion occurred in the enemy's line. A huge flame was seen the burn of the 3rd platoon, behind that trench - heavy holding schuft, party, the day. Enemy's trench mortars trained on his fire preparated in places in retaliation to our bombardment of the BIRDCAGE yesterday. Our 2nd Batt. the trenches with great few loss.	G
		10.30 pm	On enemy party of 30 or more were seen about E of T118 - On being fired on 15 patrol disappeared into the trench. On our advance to the heads as if hit. Rest shots checking into the dug out. Mining found found. - 11 Batt. CHESHIRE REGT BIRDCAGE.	

2353 Wt W2544/1454 700,000 5/15 D. D. & L. A.D.S.S./Forms/C. 2118.

Army Form C. 2118.

WAR DIARY
INTELLIGENCE SUMMARY
(Erase heading not required.)

1st/5th Batt. Cheshire Regt.

Place	Date	Hour	Summary of Events and Information	Remarks and references to Appendices
PLOEGSTEERT WOOD	28 Jany	(approx)	Tuesday. Heavy rifle & machine gun fire opened from our right by enemy. Our right company stood to arms & opened rapid fire on enemy's parapet opposite. Two men were seen on enemy's parapet opposite T113 but also apparently watching the railway line from our trenches. Enemy's front trench probably held these men, as enemy did not return the fire though the usual flares were sent up & Maxims and always turned in the wooden house (P.M.S. Row front).	J.L.
T113-120 (inclusive)		10.30am	Enemy sent up a red rocket from T115-6. No more flares after this. A small light was also observed P.M.S. opposite.	
" "	29 Jany	11.15am	An enemy biplane circled above our lines & was driven from our lines. A machine from enemies' lines & in action from her lines.	J.L.
			In BIRDCAGE. Raiding officer took out a patrol from T110 to screen of BIRDCAGE. He found T113-16 was in front of our trench had been cut, but that the enemy's listening post is still in communication trench between his two lines in front & opposite. The wire in his trenches was several places on his hidden hut of Transforty. The enemy can be actually supplied from out his trenches.	
			An enemy working party opposite T113 was fired on by our machine gun & a machine gun in H BIRDCAGE was fired on by our machine gun & given an oyster.	
		2.0am	Enemy's increased artillery activity opposite front of Brigade. No damage of any account. No firing was placed on our trenches.	
	30 Jany	12 noon	Enemy working parties were heard in & near wooden houses opposite at the BIRDCAGE. Enemy scouts found passing near T114-115 to observe working party & trenches fire opened the enemy worked.	J.L.

Army Form C. 2118.

WAR DIARY
or
INTELLIGENCE SUMMARY.
(Erase heading not required.)

11th Batt. Cheshire Regt.

Place	Date	Hour	Summary of Events and Information	Remarks and references to Appendices
PLOEGSTEERT WOOD T113-126 (inclusive)	31.8.16	12 a.m.	An Alberti's Brillant observed flying 3 enemy planes. Evening 1st biplan on our lines. Point of our front to establish posts opposite T113 and at the BIRDCAGE. Much rifle & machine gun fire. Repeating observed on PONT ROUGE ROAD. Enemy's artillery quiet. Considerable improvement is now noticeable in the trenches. — wiring to entanced pumps, etc. walls is being kept well in hand. Slime is heaved and trenches generally in Bulany's welling to the army. This week one the trenches of the R.E.	SS/1

E. J. Nevel
Major
for Commanding
11th Batt. Cheshire Regt.

75th Inf. Bde.

25th Division

11th Battn.

CHESHIRE REGIMENT,

JANUARY, 1916.

WAR DIARY
INTELLIGENCE SUMMARY

Jan, Feb, March 1916
X/5 Batt. Cheshire Regt.

Army Form C. 2118.

Places	Date	Hour	Summary of Events and Information	Remarks and references to Appendices
BOIS GRENIER WOOD	1.1.16	8.30am	The Battalion was relieved by the 1st & 8th Batt. S. Lancashire Regt. in T/13-T/20 (inclusive)	
"CRESSON" (PLACE)	1/1/16		At midnight Dec 31–Jan 1 our West firing rifle grenades in practically a few rounds together in the German prospects to greet the new year. My reply was a few desultory rifle grenades. The battalion relieved to billets at CRESSON without incident, but was during the tour and of the 2 ruins being rather little happening in its area during the day of the 2. Ruins being rather little happening but a heavy bombardment of the left if the 3.7 on 31st near RIFLE HOUSE on the afternoon of the 4th.	
	5/1/16		The 8th S. Lancs were relieved by us at 4am on the morning of the 5th. The day was quiet, the weather fair, but freezing. He they were in was reported heavily from the east, left lines and from 7pm to 9pm a machine gun opened on T.16 at intervals. Shots came from T.15 but killed no one of it.	
	6/1/16		The ESTAMINET was shelled by enemy at the edge of the wood near the falling near the road, FAW VILLA during the morning but they also enemy the 8 or 0.7 Shots came there for some time before one found to the S.E. in PICK VILLA and one from almost daily, The at the field Try between full over The road from S.E. and hay T.16 at the Hospice. If new sandbags Trench V.2/ BIRD CAGE dug out. 12.20 enemy active along the M.5 & 1 BIRD CAGE sniper dove as S. Large fires was seen at keep which have white fruits at PONT RUGE RS came or jumped of 11.2 m. but there was no sign of about them A German patrol was seen near the cutting X.9 and fired upon, supposed to have been	

WAR DIARY or INTELLIGENCE SUMMARY

Army Form C. 2118.

X1/5 Batt. Cheshire Regt.

Place	Date	Hour	Summary of Events and Information	Remarks and references to Appendices
PLOEGSTEERT WOOD	6/1/16		In rear of the trees near the crater close to the HAMPSHIRE T. trench 117 the battery took shelter, no activity by shell. DEWAR & SGT JACKSON patrolled the front of T120-119 but during the night from 9.30 to 1. Stayed out in front of the enemy. The ground was white with snow and the moon rose just in front of enemy parapet. Concealment or cover was so adopted in part of enemy parapet. ELGAR HOUSE was unoccupied. One bright red rocket seen at 6.50 pm to N of T.116, and a very bright up from ------ opposite T.116 at 7 pm.	W D K
"	7/1/16		During this day the enemy OP was constructed in principle of T.120 (or observation of BIRD CAGE. No observation of importance was thought owing to destruction of O.P. at PARK VILLA which was again shelled during the morning. Our heavies replied on the BIRDCAGE. Nothing further heard opposite T.114 reported to MG which opened fire, result not observed.	
		6.15 pm	Listening post T.114 - T120 reported nothing to hand. O point under Bde Intell [?] T.117 at T.F.M. and started at 8 pm under the German flag planted in no mans land. They was started by wire to Tree and [?] MG, and [?] upon the point parties E of BIRDCAGE and near PELERIN C. T. [?] [?] [?] [?] H am enemy E of BIRDCAGE stated to patrol to fully clad white dummy put there for dayout, on T.116. to return were captured. One of them was shown by Pigeon into that of L/Cpl [?] of 3rd WORCESTERS. The on other papers on the body worked will be forwarded when all found of [?] intelligence will be [?]	

Army Form C. 2118.

WAR DIARY
or
INTELLIGENCE SUMMARY.
(Erase heading not required.)

1st Batt. Cheshire Regt

Place	Date	Hour	Summary of Events and Information	Remarks and references to Appendices
ROSSIGNOL WOOD	7/1/16		and dated 1914. Both bodies were in an advanced state of decomposition. Work proceeded rapidly in the trenches. T116, 115 are being reconstructed with armoured trav. revetments – Two dug outs T119 begun to lay runners and start dug outs are being constructed. T118 being entered to look more like a trench but even the Dutch revetments to centre Coy HQ to the CT is receiving attention. A new C.T. is being constructed behind T120 and similar cable is being laid to GERMAN H.Q.	H.S.G.
"	8/1/16		The enemy was very quiet today. Listening post reports no hostile activity. Field grey uniform has been seen in the BIRDCAGE. S.E. of the Right mound there are some red bands about 8" high x 6" wide which appear to be part of a ruined house. Men are working behind here.	
"	9/1/16	11.30pm	At 11.30 p.m. a working party was heard off junction T/112 T/113. They spot a Verey noted on a special light was sent up by the enemy at 1.15 am after a very quiet period of 30 minutes. This may indicate return of patrol. There were more than the usual no. of flares during the afternoon along the PELERIN T.	H.S.G.
	9/1/16		This day the enemy was fairly quiet. A relief almost certainly took place on the night 8–9 inst. Runners: Still night was unusually quiet ① The snipers of the troops who occupied the line opposite up to the end of November have gone back & replaced. Three shots were fired from an enemy gun yesterday hit the sound track at the point where it cut the path & jag ups through the ridge over the CoY 119 to T116. Began to have an enemy sniper sector at the PICKET HOUSE which looks the gun set ½ at ± junction of ③ Reg'ts opened fire on T116 but did little damage to anyone is quiet. It just seems the bullets	

Army Form C. 2118.

WAR DIARY
or
INTELLIGENCE SUMMARY.
(Erase heading not required.)

Instructions regarding War Diaries and Intelligence Summaries are contained in F. S. Regs., Part II. and the Staff Manual respectively. Title pages will be prepared in manuscript.

XI th Batt. Cheshire Regt.

Place	Date	Hour	Summary of Events and Information	Remarks and references to Appendices
PLOEGSTEERT WOOD	9/1/16		positions of our former opponents. A machine gun emplacement was located at S.W. corner of BIRD CAGE and another not far away off T.117. Two snipers posts on SW corner of BIRDCAGE the other 30 yards N of well also located thus shelling opened on parapet opp T.117.	
		11.35am	Enemy biplane flying out South. 3pm Biplane over enemy lines towards WARNETON seen from 7.115. Enemy Observation balloon up to wind of day about 3 miles E of WARNETON, same type as our own at 3 PM a bright flash was seen repeatedly and signally from the basket of the balloon. A working party observed by M.G. fire at 10 P.M. and rifle suddenly opened up from BIRDCAGE about 3 AM not followed by	
	10/1/16	10pm	shell or any fire, may mean M.G. shooting at our parapet was accurate but quiet. An enemy patrol was seen near moves in front enemy alert but quiet on During night an enemy trench PP trench of BIRDCAGE. Enemy was not being observed and registra- 110 In our lines 7.115 116 117 not being observed and registered Round PP.C15 + field 1874 uniform seen in BIRDCAGE action was appeared behind German lines putties in triple file west via to Cutter + clear communication trenches PP 117 our snipers nest 15/1/16	M D A
		5.15pm	a working party in the C.T. and but one man in view in the sight. There was a little sniping during the day a little sniping by us which usually MG fire fairly quiet day at night apparently afraid to use own guns considerable through the night vigorously shelled of our own guns considerable smoke was seen above on enemy trenches. Spies have been issued in roses	
	11/1/16		sandbags filled irregularly in the front trench of the BIRD CAGE	M D C

2353 Wt. W2544/1454 700,000 5/15 D. D. & L. A.D.S.S./Forms/C. 2118.

WAR DIARY / INTELLIGENCE SUMMARY

Army Form C. 2118.

1st Batt. Cheshire Regt.

Place	Date	Hour	Summary of Events and Information	Remarks and references to Appendices
PLOEGSTEERT WOOD	11/1/16		During night a patrol under 2nd Lieut Officer went through garden & ruins in front of PICKET HOUSE. Enemy were found very strong on LE GHEER ROAD. A large house behind the white house on the LE GHEER-WARNETON road is suspected of being a headquarters. Several cyclist orderlies were observed coming & going with considerable activity near the house. We were shelled intermittently during the day, transport was heard during the night on the same road.	
	2-3 p.m.		Sandbags (6) were sent over near PICKET HOUSE in reply to one dud. Was observed by the bombing officer. The approx. portion of the Sansay-Turlup was located. The bombing was relieved by the 8th Batt South Lancs at 9.0 a.m.	M.D.K.
	12/1/16		Rest of the Bn. The day in the trenches was exceptionally quiet. Activity was confined chiefly to sniping and occasional shells such as that which fell near the junction in HUNTERS AVENUE and behind ashes to try to cut our left front to be joining a large proportion of enemy artillery attention doubtless in order to a battery in the enemy's lines approximately (not known exactly) yards behind the centre front line, on the very slightly cut off the cellars used [unclear]... was [unclear] which is the house known [unclear] [unclear] and his [unclear] was quiet [unclear] [unclear] was not [unclear] until the night and all the BURNIE ROW... [unclear] a few shells were [unclear] in a range of T.115. Wing in front of T.115 – M. Picket's dugouts were [unclear] damaged. [unclear] by [unclear] [unclear] [unclear] transport [unclear] [unclear] [unclear] [unclear] in answer [unclear] Rations [unclear] [unclear] weather has been good and [unclear] [unclear] [unclear] the roots are getting [unclear] the trenches in getting drier.	

WAR DIARY or INTELLIGENCE SUMMARY

Army Form C. 2118.

1st Batt. Cheshire Regt.

Place	Date	Hour	Summary of Events and Information	Remarks and references to Appendices
CRESLOW (billets)	12/1/16	9am	The battalion returned to usual reserve billets and found that CRESLOW and neighbouring villages had been shelled during their absence, probably by 4-5" hows. The town in billets was very quiet. The only incident to record was that two small shells fell close to CRESLOW on the 14th at about 3pm.	H. D. K.
"	15/1/16	9am	The battalion relieved the 8th Batt. South Lancs in the trenches (113-120 inclusive)	H. D. K.
	16/1/16		The day was quiet save for activity with rifle grenades and trench mortars at 11.15 p.m. two bombs exploding at T.117 were located a battery [?] at PIC QUET HOUSE was suspected also the presence of a German patrol our wire but very light failed to disclose him. Enemy took up important position opposite A though hostile snipers were quiet. A full moon enabled rapid [?] on front during the night. At T.115 enemy contacted [?] patrol went out in front of T.115 enemy put [?] very heavy light notest up during the night. A [?] party of PICQUET HO was brought by our front [?] [?] my wire began [?] very very [?] no [?] during the day an enemy airplane flew [?] the company trench passed over VI S A 3. At [?] shape 5 ft [?] [?] along [?]	H. D. K.
	19/1/16		The day was quiet and T.114 except enemy sniper firing on S/L 7.116 very active during the [?] of [?] the enemy was [?] during the day. Very [?] after S/L T.115 our [?] [?] a [?] [?] [?] [?] of [?] [?] the 7th Batt [?] accounted by the [?] [?] [?] [?] to the [?] [?] the 7th Batt [?] [?] [?] enemy 2.30am [?] [?] [?] [?] relieved by 1/2 10am [?] [?] [?] two guns 15 [?] / SALIENT [?] [?] DEERS HUT	

WAR DIARY or INTELLIGENCE SUMMARY

Army Form C. 2118.

XI:th Batt. Cheshire Regt.

Place	Date	Hour	Summary of Events and Information	Remarks and references to Appendices
PLOEGSTEERT WOOD	19/1/16		To LE GHEER was heavily bombarded by all calibres & German trench mortars. T.111 and T.110 up to main supports were extremely heavily shelled. Our trenches were practically unaffected. From 4:30 pm till 5:15 pm on a front of about 440 yds. They opened all 4:30 & 4:45 pm 6:00 pm a hell of fire. They kept heavy burst about the line & rang heavy but the night H.G. fire continued from 6:30 to 6 am (24Hrs) - Specially all night a M.G. was located to the front from which the fire was most difficult [to?] deal with & which swept the parapet (either at T:22 D.3.5) from toe to... later bound to be not far ... Our M.G. but T... 113 + 114 at 4:50 pm - 9:PM 11:5 - 9.40 PM and CAGE replied till 5:15 when firing from M.L. died... 91 were evident that... while speaking, no attack from the trenches, 113 - 7:20 especially they were undoubtedly from the enemy lines opp. T114 - an attack... the enemy were very little [?] Our trenches suffered very little loss casualties being but one of B Coy. one... wounded at C... one slightly injured no T:115 one very slightly ... ... on at 6 - the enemy fire about 9:15 am ... They ... Verey lights & pushed a patrol to...	M.D.K.
	20/1/16			

Army Form C. 2118.

WAR DIARY
or
INTELLIGENCE SUMMARY.
(Erase heading not required.)

XIth Batt. Cheshire Regt

Place	Date	Hour	Summary of Events and Information	Remarks and references to Appendices
PLOEGSTEERT WOOD	20/4/16	9 am	The night 20-21st was very quiet and an enemy patrol was inspected. Enemy aircraft were busy during the morning at 10 am by Capt. was seen moved (sic, dirty white) over MESSINES at 10.15 at 10.30 am & 11.15 am a [illegible] and another... towards WARNETON. One fired on by No. 11 on... [illegible] ...PICKET HOUSE ... DON'T RODGE Rd at 8.30 am ...	
		2 pm	... T.114 J.115 ...	
		6 pm	... Hdqr RATION ...	
			...	
	21/4/16	2.45 pm	...	

Army Form C. 2118.

WAR DIARY
or
INTELLIGENCE SUMMARY.
(Erase heading not required.)

XIth Batt. Cheshire Regt.

Place	Date	Hour	Summary of Events and Information	Remarks and references to Appendices
ROUGESTREET WOOD	21/1/16		During afternoon 10 rifle grenades sent into BIRDCAGE from T119 shewed no retaliation, possibly enemy R.G. stands moved opp T113 after demonstration on the 19th. Our M.G.s were active during the night and dispersed working parties at fords PICKET HO. and in BIRDCAGE left of 118. BIRDCAGE left of 118 sniper chagrined as a sandbag. BH sniper claim to have bagged a German sniper. Enemy's usual artillery activity continues — Relief of 1st to 3rd trenches of sub-sectors effected satisfactorily - [illegible] — [illegible]	H.D.K.
"	22/1/16		BIRDCAGE L112 S J112 right burned [illegible] and showed [illegible] have been repaired during the previous nights. During the night our Enemy patrol was seen traverse his trenches opposite T117. The patrol was dispersed by rifle fire. A red light has been shewn every [illegible] opposite T110. At 7.30 p.m. an enemy working party at V.22.c.33. was dispersed by our machine gun fire. At 12.30 am Seven enemy rifle grenades fell near GERMAN HOUSE. Four of the seven failed to explode. Our artillery most successfully silenced [illegible] movements to [illegible] the enemy lines and practically quietened enemy in MG. [illegible]	
"	23/1/16		Enemy's activity increased. Retaliatory rifle fire, from the enemy's trenches [illegible] the patrol movements from T119 [illegible] the patrol [illegible] between B.S. corner of BIRDCAGE [illegible]	G.W. BIRDGE

Army Form C. 2118.

WAR DIARY
INTELLIGENCE SUMMARY
(Erase heading not required.)

X1=(S)Batt. Cheshire Regt.

Place	Date	Hour	Summary of Events and Information	Remarks and references to Appendices
PLOEGSTEERT WOOD T.113 - 120 (in Section)	23.7.16		Inhabitation patrol was out on artillery front on this morning. Enemy and our T.M. was busy. Five Stripped and one M.E. Trench Mortar burst on the Parapet. The latter was seen to cause wreck. At 4.15 p.m. an Hotchkiss in Barrel was almost seen opened fire on this morning pass, but no opposition was offered. Several times during the night red lights were started by the enemy and also enemy who was informed by watching the men. The next light never replied to on rifle or signal. Many star lights sent up to the front from his support and near front line his front trenches.	CP3
	24.7.16		At 7 a.m. the Battalion was relieved by the 8th Batt S. Lancashire Regt in T.113-120. Took over billets in Brigade Reserve with HeadQuarters at CRESLOW. Orders received for the Division (25th) Move back into Corps Reserve, the line being taken over by the 9th & 10th Brigades. The Battalion moved off at 1 pm. to an area (STRAZEELE) in the 2nd Corps Rest area, and came hit by making all Preparations for the movement. Advance party of the HE Batt Royal Scots moved at 12.30 into billets.	CP3
	25.7.16		The Battalion marched to camp LA CRECHE leaving here in the morning. Reached Strazeele during this Somb 115 officers and commenced work.	CP3
	26.7.16		Scattered - Officers killed 2nd Lieut Taylor. Officers slightly wounded 2nd Lieut Mountain Gun Officers wounded NCO's train killed in other ranks 26, wounded 67. Other ranks lost (2)-

Army Form C. 2118.

WAR DIARY
INTELLIGENCE SUMMARY.
(Erase heading not required.)

XIth Batt. Cheshire Regt.

Place	Date	Hour	Summary of Events and Information	Remarks and references to Appendices
LA CRECHE	26.1.16	9.30am	The Battalion arrived at LA CRECHE and went into billets in the village for the night.	Est.
	27.1.16	9am	The above XIth Bat. after a long march, 11th Battalion arrived at STRAZEELE at 1 pm. Some permanent billets consisting of several farm houses and buildings were taken over. Division Head Quarters was situated at MERRIS, Brigade Head Quarters (75th) at STRAZEELE, and Batt. Head Quarters at a farm about half a mile W. of STRAZEELE on the STRAZEELE – HAZEBROUCK Road. The other units of the 75th Brigade i.e. the 8th Border Regt. and the 2nd and 8th Batts. S. Lancashire Regt. occupied billets in the neighbourhood of STRAZEELE. The 74th Brigade was billeted around OUTTERSTENE and the 74th Brigade around LA CRECHE – The Divisional Artillery was at CAESTRE –	Est.
STRAZEELE			On the first night after arrival at STRAZEELE the men were just complete, seeing as been doing Except Clearing up, improving billets etc.	
	31.1.16		Lt.Col. W.R.H. Brown proceeded to England on leave, and Major E.G. Hind assumed command of the Battalion.	Est.

75th Inf. Bde.

25th Division.

<u>11th Battn</u>.

<u>CHESHIRE REGIMENT</u>,

<u>FEBRUARY, 1916</u>.

Army Form C. 2118.

WAR DIARY
or
INTELLIGENCE SUMMARY.

XIth Batt. Cheshire Regt.

1.2.16		Transport commenced 5 days instructional work during the morning. The 11/12 came into billets at night by 3 pm 9th Division relieved 15th Battalion from houses and as ordered accordingly.	
2.2.16			
STRAZEELE 9.2.16	10 am	The Battalion was inspected on a road march by H.M. 2nd Army Commander General Sir Herbert Plumer, on the STRAZEELE – FLETRE Road. Brigadier General Woodward, Bde had commanded the 75th Brigade carried the formation returned with the Command and returned to England. Brigadier General Jenkins attached commanding the Bgde.	
10.2.16		The Battalion was inspected in Column front by Field Marshal Earl Kitchener, on the STRAZEELE – CAESTRE Road.	
	11.30 am	Nine Officers and 150 men proceeded to the Divisional Grenade School OUTTERSTEENE & with an a Course taken with the German Hanovermen (opportunity for effective hand fire) – Intimation received that Capt. F.W. Lawson, who came out to France with the Battalion, had relinquished his commission on account ill health, and reported Gazette 22.1.16 –	
12.2.16		An officers and a proportion of the ranks attended a lecture on musketry by Lt. Col. Richardson y/to 2nd Army Sniping School.	
13.2.16		The Battalion received orders that half of the men who were unfit to have rifles. This list of names were enclosed in register by Lt. Col. recommended by YPRES.	

2353   Wt. W2544/1454 700,000 5/15 D. D. & L. A.D.S.S./Forms/C. 2118.

75th Inf. Bde.

25th Division

11th Battn.

CHESHIRE REGIMENT,

MARCH, 1916.

Army Form C. 2118.

WAR DIARY

INTELLIGENCE SUMMARY

(Erase heading not required.)

11th Batt. Cheshire Regt.

Instructions regarding War Diaries and Intelligence Summaries are contained in F. S. Regs., Part II. and the Staff Manual respectively. Title pages will be prepared in manuscript.

Place	Date	Hour	Summary of Events and Information	Remarks and references to Appendices
STRAZEELE	4.3.16	12 noon	The Battalion was to have been inspected by the Commander-in-Chief but owing to the bad weather the parade was cancelled until later moment.	
	10.3.16		Orders having been received for the Division to join the 3rd Army, the Battalion marched to STRAZEELE and was billeted for the night at PECQUEUR, proceeding on the following day to NEDONCHELLE.	
NEDONCHELLE	11.3.16		Here it remained in billets till the 16th inst. During this period Company & Battalion training was carried out.	
VALHUON	16.3.16	9 a.m.	The Battalion marched to VALHUON arriving at about 2 p.m. and took over billets vacated by the 9th Batt. Wiltshire Regt.	
	23.3.16		H.Q. Company, No.2 Company and ?? became Brigade Reserve 9th Sherwood Foresters 2nd.... R. XVII Corps. Saturday the afternoon.	
	25.3.16		The scheme (Instn. No.01) carried the Brigade to the Machine Gun front line. Brigade join for Hostile	
TINQUES	29.3.16 (?)		.... vacated by the 9th Batt. Northumberland Fusiliers .... The Companies have billets at ?? The ...... Battn HQT	

Army Form C. 2118.

WAR DIARY
INTELLIGENCE SUMMARY.
(Erase heading not required.)

XI:th Batt. Cheshire Regt.

Place	Date	Hour	Summary of Events and Information	Remarks and references to Appendices
TINTUES	31-3-16	11 AM	The Battalion was inspected at Company training by the Commander-in-Chief, General Sir Douglas Haig.	See [?]

W.P. Oldham Lt Col
Commanding
11th Batt. Cheshire Regt

75th Inf. Bde.

25th Division.

11th Battn.

CHESHIRE REGIMENT,

1ST TO 19TH A P R I L, 1 9 1 6.

Confidential

War Diary

of

11ᵗʰ (S) Batt. Cheshire Regiment.

from 1-4-16 to 3-6-16

the months of April + May

J. R. L. Aspinall Lt. Col.
Commdg 11ᵗʰ Batt Cheshire Regt.

WAR DIARY
INTELLIGENCE SUMMARY

Army Form C. 2118.

Apr 1916 XXII Vol 5.6
11(S) Batt Sherwood Rest[?]

Place	Date	Hour	Summary of Events and Information	Remarks and references to Appendices
TINQUES	1/4/16		The morning was spent Training - specialists (i.e. Grenadiers, Lewis Gunners, Machine Gunners) being under their specialist Officers. In the afternoon Colonel Catton (Commanding 2nd South Lancs Regt, attached 7th Brigade 9th (S) 18th Ind Bde) judged a Platoon Competition in which Platoon No 7 12 & 16 took part, intended to be best Platoon in the Battalion. The Platoons were Commanded by 2/Lt M.S. Synnott (OC7). The Judge remarked that they were nearly all No 16. No 7 + 16 were the best & emphasised that competition whilst to decide which No 7 + 16 were the best & emphasised that competition in itself was fine turnout. The competition was held at BETHENCOURT	C.F.H
-do-	2/4/16		Divine Service was held for C of E, Nonconformists & Roman Catholics.	
-do-	3/4/16		The Battalion Attack scheme was practised in BOIS-du-HEROM BUS about 1½ miles S.W. of TINQUES. Spectators chance was held during the afternoon and in addition a NCO's class under the Adjutant. To having of Lt Col Bett, well specialists entrained & all outstanding men were given some communication drill by the adjutant. In the evening Major Evans 2nd in Command of 2nd S. Lancs Regt gave a lecture musketry in the Ecole hall Major Evans May 15.	5 P. 11 sheet

Army Form C. 2118.

WAR DIARY
or
INTELLIGENCE SUMMARY.
(Erase heading not required.)

Place	Date	Hour	Summary of Events and Information	Remarks and references to Appendices
CHELERS	12/9/16		On the 11th inst. Batt. Hd Qrs moved into the CHATEAU at CHELERS and in the evening a lecture was given to the Officers N.C.O's on "Nystagmus & Nystagmoid". Major L.H.K Finch of the Cheshire Regt. joined for duty as 2nd in command of the Battalion vice Major E.G Freed appointed A.P.M at GHQ. 2nd Coy of the Batt'n attacked a demonstration aft of Flammenwerfer in the afternoon about ½ mile E of ROELLECOURT. Men obtained billets at TINQUES.	CF 13
	13/9/16			CF 14
	14/9/16		In the 14th inst. the Brigade was inspected by Lt-Gen'l the Hon'ble Sir Julian Byng KCMG, CB, commanding the XVII Corps. The Battalion received praise from the Corps Commander on the fine appearance they acting one more compliment to an all ready long list. Its in noteworthy that during its period of rest the Batt'n has been picked out from the rest of the Brigade and its allowance remarked upon by some General who has inspected it. eg Brig Gen'l STRAZEELE by Lt Kitchener by Gen Plumer and by Lt Army by General Jacqueson command II Corps and at CHELERS by 6,000 NDE Corps.	CF 8

Army Form C. 2118.

WAR DIARY
or
INTELLIGENCE SUMMARY
(Erase heading not required).

Instructions regarding War Diaries and Intelligence Summaries are contained in F. S. Regs., Part II, and the Staff Manual respectively. Title Pages will be prepared in manuscript.

Place	Date	Hour	Summary of Events and Information	Remarks and references to Appendices
CHELERS	15/4/16		Battalion outpost scheme in morning, E of CHELERS.	
"	16/4/16		8 Officers of the Batt'n went by motor lorry to inspect new trench haunts in NEUVILLE – ST – VAAST. Very fine day.	
"	17/4/16		4 Officers of the Batt'n went by lorry to NEUVILLE – ST – VAAST. Companies carried out training under O.C. Coys.	
"	18/4/16		Training under Coy Comdrs. 5 Officers attended a musketry demonstration at BUNÉVILLE in morning. Brigade bombing competition in afternoon, indifferent weather. We did not do as well as we might, but succeeded in beating the 9th Gordons for 15th place in competition ("dummy grenates").	
"	19/4/16		Unusually wet day. Training under Coy Comdrs, but very difficult training out on account of rain. Preparations for an Inter Platoon Tournament.	

75th Inf. Bde.

25th Division

11th Battn.

CHESHIRE REGIMENT,

20th APRIL to 1st JUNE, 1916.

WAR DIARY or INTELLIGENCE SUMMARY

Army Form C. 2118.

1/1st Cheshires (25 Div)

20/4 - 1/6/16

Place	Date	Hour	Summary of Events and Information	Remarks and references to Appendices
	29/4/16	10 a.m.	Battalion marched to Ecoivres, waited in billets (huts) there for darkness, and moved into Brigade Reserve at Neuville - St - Vaast about 8 p.m. relieving 5/ South Staffs Regt. C & D coys lived in cellars, and A & B coys each in a huge cave about 50 feet below ground. Very unpleasant existence, but fairly safe. Battn. H.Q. at "Church corner" in the village. Transport at A.C.Q. During following days the Battn. furnished strong working parties for strengthening of main line of defence, which was in a wretched state, much from neglect, partly from heavy rain. occasional shelling in both sides, but nothing serious.	
Bn. H.Q. Neuville St Vaast. Front line.	27/5/16		Battalion moved into front line at 9.pm. 10th Cheshires occupied the front line. Bn. in Bn.Reserve, quiet night.	WCB
Ecoivres	6/5/16		The Battalion marched to Divisional Reserve after a very interesting 6 days in the trenches, the weather was splendid and all ranks	WCB

WAR DIARY or INTELLIGENCE SUMMARY

Army Form C. 2118.

Place	Date	Hour	Summary of Events and Information	Remarks and references to Appendices
ECOIVRES	6/5/16		in excellent spirits. The line being new to us, put us at a considerable disadvantage and on the 2nd night in (28/[Sept]) the Enemy made their few interesting, evidently having arranged a organised bombing attack upon all our saps, at different periods through the night. Our Coy bombers really did very well, and silenced them at all points, he lost 6 casualties. On the morning of the 28th 2nd Vickers was sniped his head below Sanny his life. The bullet glancing inwards + inflicting a scalp wound. All day on the 29th we learned the enemy saps through periscopes and aeroplane photographs, and the Bombing Officer planned a retaliatory diversion by means of Rifle Grenades, Trench Guns and volley throwing by Service Section Bombers. It was entirely successful, and we suffered no casualties. We had one man sniped on the 30th and by that date had the enemy snipers well in hand. Most difficult lines to have acquainted with owing to being so shot up by craters and saps. Quite a maze of the latter. East of the craters Nothing of importance occurred during the remainder of the tour, we always took the initiative in bombing + repeatedly bombed	

WAR DIARY or INTELLIGENCE SUMMARY

Army Form C. 2118.

Place	Date	Hour	Summary of Events and Information	Remarks and references to Appendices
Ecoivres	6/5/16		The enemy rd. 2 stun shots over (with 1 gas) to intimate Saperis to the Corons from what is the Cathedral. This and contains no steeple. It makes a most demoralising noise however. On the night of 2/3rd we expected an enemy mine to go then Craters at 0630 and 0700, as a Canadian engineer reported the Germans as having stopped work in the shaft, in which our working party in close proximity, but enemy started work again. The 8th Borders relieved us at 6.0 p.m. on 3rd May. The Battalion Road to arm - Parallel VIII until 2nd S. Lancs were in Billets Neuville St. Vaast when we marched into Ecoivres. The men going into spacious huts. They all seem very happy, which is but natural, for the weather is fine and everywhere is Rest and Peace and Sweet.	Nil
Ecoivres	8/5/16		On the night of 8th, we had a concert arranged for in the men the R.F.C. assisting, proved a very enjoyable evening. On the night of the 7th the Commanding Officer gave a Smoking Concert to the Officers of the 11th Cheshires, held in the Chateau	Nil

BSD - B. M351.22/41. 12/15. 5000.

WAR DIARY or INTELLIGENCE SUMMARY

Army Form C. 2118.

Place	Date	Hour	Summary of Events and Information	Remarks and references to Appendices
Ecoivres	8/5/16		Very successful. Remainder are of old fledgeling days	WR
Neuville Saint Vaaste	9/5/16	6 am	Relieved 8th Borders in front line, relief being complete at 12 midnight very wet. Quiet night, about 8 a.m. followed by a long bombardment by both sides & mines. About 3 mines were exploded on our left (officers) Casualties came in for last 9 pt.	WR
"	11/5/16		Night yesterday, enemy registered with Rifle Grenades on O.63 and O.65 and in reply to our return fire, in midnight sent over about 25, obtaining direct hits, unfortunately knocking out one of our machine guns. Bombing officer arranged a nice stoke for O.63 and O.65 which was entirely successful. Weather today (11th) fine but cloudy.	WR
Neuville St Vaaste. Rt. Russen	13/5/16		The 8th Borders relieved us on the night of 16/17th. We had quiet an active tour and several useful patrols were carried out. On the 16th we received the following from G.O.C. 75th Bde "The G.O.C. 75th Bde has received the following from the G.O.C. Division, "The G.O.C. Division is pleased to see the aggressive action on the part of the 11th Cheshire Regt. By such means complete ascendancy must be gained over the enemy. Consequently the more numerous similar enterprises are, the more pleased will the G.O.C. be." The weather now is delightful, and indeed lately we…	WR

BSD - B. M351. 22/11. 12/15. 5000.

WAR DIARY or INTELLIGENCE SUMMARY

Army Form C. 2118.

Place	Date	Hour	Summary of Events and Information	Remarks and references to Appendices
Neuville	19/5/16		Our casualties list two were principally caused by rifle grenades and trench mortars. Our Stokes guns and T.M's were active and called forth a good deal of retaliation. The enemy sending salvoes of 77cm and 4.5 shells into our Safford line. The lot two men killed and ten wounded.	N/B
Fosseux	20/5/16		We relieved the 5th Border. Dick Heard to set out of the caves again.	N/B
	21/5/16		At about 11.0 P.M. Lieut Berche was hit by shrapnel from an aerial torpedo. – 0.65. He sustained a fractured skull and had unnecessary convulsions after sent to Field Ambulance at 2 a.m.	
Ecoivres	26th		Borders relieved us regal BF 24/25a. We had a quiet uneventful tour except for Moushes tapping about 3 hear is propressing favourably. Our Stokes guns did good shooting. – one afternoon knocking out 4 Snipers plate, the O.P. and a machine gun emplacement on B.6.	
MINGOVAL	1/6/16		The Battalion branched out here arriving about 12.00 midnight Weather fine and clear.	N/B

BSD – B/M851/22/11. 12/15 5000.

75th Inf. Bde.

25th Division

11th Battn.

CHESHIRE REGIMENT,

3rd to 30th JUNE, 1916.

Army Form C. 2118.

WAR DIARY
or
INTELLIGENCE SUMMARY.
(Erase heading not required.)

Instructions regarding War Diaries and Intelligence Summaries are contained in F. S. Regs., Part II. and the Staff Manual respectively. Title pages will be prepared in manuscript.

Place	Date	Hour	Summary of Events and Information	Remarks and references to Appendices
TINQUES	5/5/16		Battalion was exercised in Batt. Drill arranged the training during the morning. All specialist classes were held, also the Warrant Officers class. Afternoon the Batt. took part in a Brigade scheme — and competed in practicing the Advance at Night. Between and Bivouacked.	
TINQUES	6/6/16 7/6/16 8/6/16		Next 3 days were spent in having General talks on the various subject Corps Tactical attacks and also 2 wonders visited by being shown and inspected with the TINQUES Station. On the morning of the 8/6/16 O.C. Corps visited and in Co.fs Line — Foufrechamps (fine) attached was W. Affulla but probably 6 Me ARRAS - SOUCHEZ Road. 6 M^e 6/16 visited - Lt Col R. L. Ashwell D.S.O received command of the Batt. after 5 months sick leave in England.	Cf.
do	9/6/16		Divine Service held for the demonstration. On the 10th inst. the Batt. moved into billets at CHELERS which had been found vacated by the 2nd Royal Irish Rifles. During the move the Batt. was practiced as forming the Advance Guard to a Brigade in contact with the enemy.	

WAR DIARY or INTELLIGENCE SUMMARY

Army Form C. 2118.

Place	Date	Hour	Summary of Events and Information	Remarks and references to Appendices
Ninqoval	3/6/16		Yesterday 2nd was spent by the Bn in starting the tents with much as they arrived very wet and were, and pitching them under a wood. the rest of the day was spent in removing all signs of the trenches, and foot ball. Today 3rd was spent in training under Company arrangement, chiefly from 6.30 to 7.15, 9.45 to 12.30, bayonet fighting, swedish drill, musketry, company drill, 2.15 to 3.15, specialists training. The band are hard at work and are really good, and are appreciated by all ranks. Our total casualties whilst in the trenches at Neuville St Vaaste were 2 officers wounded, other ranks, 6 killed, 3 died of wounds and 19 wounded.	

R J Aspinall Lt Col
Comm 9. 11th Batt Cheshire Regt

Army Form C. 2118

WAR DIARY
or
INTELLIGENCE SUMMARY

(Erase heading not required.)

11. Cheshires
Vol 7

Place	Date	Hour	Summary of Events and Information	Remarks and references to Appendices
MINGOVAL	4.vi.16		The Battalion was still in MINGOVAL under Canvas, and on this date was commenced a period of preparing Training in 'Offensive warfare'. The Transport was inspected by B.G. General Jenkins, Commd'g 75th Brigade, who expressed his satisfaction at the turn out & condition of the animals. Notification was received that Lt H. E. Dewar's name appeared in the Birthday Honours list as a recipient of the Military Cross. Lt Dewar had received previous commendation for excellent work in reconnaissance while the Batt'n occupied the Trenches in PLOEGSTEERT. This first recognition of the Battalion was a matter of gratification to all ranks.	
	6.vi.16		News was received that Lt Col G.G. Burke, who received a severe head wound from an aerial Torpedo (Minenwerfer) on a fortnight ago while in the trenches at NEUVILLE-ST-VAAST, had succumbed on June 4th 1916 at the No II Red Cross Hospital at ROUEN. This news was received with universal regret, as Lt Burke was not only a most capable Officer, but was a great favourite with all ranks.	
	7.vi.16		News was received that Field Marshal Earl Kitchener K.G. had been drowned at sea on the night of June 5th, while being conveyed on a Battleship to Russia on a special mission to the Czar. The Commanding Officer announced this natural loss to the Battalion assembled on Parade, laying especial stress on the connection	
	8.vi.16		of this great Soldier with the New Armies, of which the Battalion forms a unit, and which will be known to countless generations hereafter, as they are known today, as Kitchener's Army.	

Army Form C. 2118

WAR DIARY
or
INTELLIGENCE SUMMARY
(Erase heading not required.)

Instructions regarding War Diaries and Intelligence Summaries are contained in F.S. Regs., Part II. and the Staff Manual respectively. Title Pages will be prepared in manuscript.

Place	Date	Hour	Summary of Events and Information	Remarks and references to Appendices
MINGOVAL	9.vi.16		The Battalion took part in a big Brigade Field day, entailing a long march to & from the trenches area, and at the conclusion of operations was inspected by Major General Bainbridge who recently succeeded Major Genl Beauchamp D'oran in command of the 25th Division. The inspecting Officer remarked on the fine physique of the men, and made tribute to their steadiness in the Ranks. It was obvious that he was pleased with everything as he did not make a single disparaging allusion. The Transport Officer (Lt Hughes) was also commended for the condition of his animals, the cleanliness of the harness, & general efficient turn out. About this period the Rev J.H. Kidd, Army Chaplain (C. of E.), was attached to the Battn. During the whole of its fortnights stay at MINGOVAL the Battalion was constantly exercising at company, Battn, Brigade & Divisional Training. The latter included operations of a most interesting but a very arduous character. The operations daily extended over the greater portion of the day & included a march of from 6 to 10 miles each way, to and from the manoeuvre ground. The weather was most unpropitious, & all which & drenching rain were continuous throughout its fortnight. The men of the Battalion, however showed splendid morale, and maintained the most excellent spirit.	
MONTES-en-TERNOIS	14.vi.16		On June 14th the Battalion moved by march route from MINGOVAL to MONTES-EN-TERNOIS. All doubtful marchers preceded the mainly in easy stages, and the men of 12 miles or muddy roads were completed without a single man falling out. Information was received that no Sergt Walton has	

WAR DIARY or INTELLIGENCE SUMMARY

Army Form C. 2118

Place	Date	Hour	Summary of Events and Information	Remarks and references to Appendices
			been awarded the Military Medal. The gallant conduct of Sergt Walton was brought to notice by the Commanding Officer, for disregard of danger and devotion to duty in going first out of the trenches and superintending their removal to a place of safety in a particularly vicious attack with bombs and aerial torpedoes made by the Germans on this B/n post in the front line trenches at NEUVILLE-ST-VAAST. This was the first recommendation of a N.C.O. that received recognition in the Campaign, and the honour was highly appreciated by the Battalion in whom credit is taken by Sergt Walton's gallantry. Unfortunately Sergt Walton was recently evacuated to England on medical grounds, so the C.O. was disappointed of honouring the decoration on him in the presence of his comrades. Capt Yates who was hurriedly down by the same arrival reports which hurried Yates in the case of 2nd/Lieut Pewche, was admitted into Hospital suffering from shellfire, the result of severe concussion. Distance marched: 12 miles.	
VILLERS d'HOPITAL	15.VI.16		Owing to the introduction of the Daylight Saving scheme in France, an hour's rest was lost to the Battalion on the night of May 15th/16th, and on the morning of the 16th Reveille was sounded at 4 a.m., on 5 a.m. new time. At 8 a.m. the Battalion marched to VILLERS d'HOPITAL, a distance of 12 miles, arriving at its destination at 12.25 mid-day. During the march the Battalion filed past B.G. Genl Jenkins, commanding 75th Brigade, who commented on its fine physique & appearance, and especially with regard to its cleanliness of personality. While marching through the town of FREVENT	

1875 Wt. W593/826 1,000,000 4/15 J.B.C. & A. A.D.S.S./Forms/C. 2118.

WAR DIARY
or
INTELLIGENCE SUMMARY
(Erase heading not required.)

Army Form C. 2118

Place	Date	Hour	Summary of Events and Information	Remarks and references to Appendices
	1916			
VILLERS L'HOPITAL	17th June		A General Officer (identity unknown) stopped the Adjutant who was riding in rear of Battn, & asked him what Regiment it was, and to what Formation it belonged. On receiving particulars, he made a warm encomium on its appearance, and expressed his opinion that the body of men was very fine; and in paying tribute to their soldierly appearance, said it was the best Battalion of the kind unless that he had seen. He also said that the Officers must be proud of commanding such a splendid corps, and that the men must be equally proud of Officers who could bring them to such a pitch of Training and Discipline to which they had obviously been subjected. On this date the Commanding Officer received orders to accompany a party of Seven Officers to make a reconnaissance of Trenches N. of _____. On the night of the 17th & 18th the Battalion changed station by night march, reaching billets at BERNAVILLE at 2am	
BERNAVILLE	18th June		After a rest of 8 hours, the Battalion resumed its march. During the day Divine Service was held in an orchard by the Revd Kidd, who has recently placed in spiritual charge, leaving BERNAVILLE at 11.30 p.m. the Battn marched with the Brigade to ST OUEN, which Town it reached about 3am. The Town was overcrowded with Troops, no billets were dispensed with & a Bivouac was formed in a large Orchard S. of the Railway. Fortunately the weather conditions were delightful, & a thoroughly good rest was enjoyed, and all ranks appeared as fresh as paint when they turned out at 10am on the 19th for their early morning run.	

WAR DIARY or INTELLIGENCE SUMMARY

Army Form C. 2118

Place	Date 1916	Hour	Summary of Events and Information	Remarks and references to Appendices
ST. OUEN	June 19th		Lieut Hay of the 75th Field Ambulance assumed Medical charge of the Battn, vice Lt Parsons R.A.M.C. who was received into hospital. 2nd Lt D. Twigg reported for duty, from the 3rd Battn. Capt J.W.H. Atkill was concurred by the Commanding Officer, at the interview J.S.O.C. for making a letter concerning an application for a transfer in insult in improper terms. The censure to be noted & against the name of this officer in his records at the War Office. At 7.30 p.m on this date the Battalion moved from its Bivouac to Billets at SURCAMPS and its neighbourhood; C & D companies being quartered in the village of that name, while H.Q.-qrs and A and B company were established at the Farm of LA HAIE, about ½ a mile distant. The following officers joined the Royal Flying Corps about this date : 2/Lt Stead, 2/Lt Exley. Capt Hughes was appointed to the Machine Gun Corps and proceeded to England to undergo instruction at the M.G. School at Grantham.	
		22h	Lt Hay, R.A.M.C. was placed in Medical Charge of the Battalion, vice Lt Parsons R.A.M.C.	
		24h	The Battalion's stay at ST OUEN was a very agreeable one, and the weather was on the whole fine. A fine agricultural area was available for training purposes, and schemes of attack, outpost &c were carried out. The surrounding country in this neighbourhood is very beautiful. On the 26th Capt J.W.H. Atkill was reprimanded by the G.O.C Division for writing a letter of an insubordinate character to his Commanding Officer. Capt Atkill was warned that a repetition of this offence would entail trial by Court Martial.	

WAR DIARY or INTELLIGENCE SUMMARY

Army Form C. 2118

Place	Date 1916	Hour	Summary of Events and Information	Remarks and references to Appendices
THIALMAS	25th June		On the night of June 24/25th the Battalion marched in Brigade, by night to THIALMAS, arriving at their destination at 2.30 am. Distance was about 15 miles, hilly and very heavy roads, extremely dark atmosphere oppressive and a heavy drizzle at times. The march was rendered more trying by constant halts & checks. A great number of men in the Brigade fell out from exhaustion, but the 11th Cheshire Regt showed considerable steadiness and entered into their new billets with only one of their number not present, and half an hour afterwards even this one man had rejoined. 2nd Lt. Bewley reported for duty from the 3rd Battalion.	
	28th		On the night of June 27/28th the Battalion marched in Brigade to TOUTENCOURT and took up quarters in hutments. The halting ground was much crowded, and Transport delayed by bad roads. However the Travelling Kitchens arrived about 2.30 am, and soup was provided on prior to the men turning in. During this month a Despatch was published in the London Gazette and the following Officers & N.C.O's received mention:— Lt Pocock, Capt Murray, Col Sergt Major Vaught, Sergt Lythgoe, Sergt Jackson, Cpl Clarke, & Cpl Capden. A special recommendation for recognition had been made to the Commander-in-Chief in the case of Sergt Jackson, for conspicuous gallantry in throwing into a place of safety bombs, with fuses in ignition, that had fallen near his comrades and which, had it not been for his presence of mind, would have caused most serious & most probably fatal results. Incidents of this nature occurred on more than one occasion whilst the Battalion was in trenches at PLOEGSTEERT WOOD.	

WAR DIARY
or
INTELLIGENCE SUMMARY

(Erase heading not required.)

Army Form C. 2118

Place	Date	Hour	Summary of Events and Information	Remarks and references to Appendices
TOUTENCOURT	29th June		This date found the Battalion in Hutment at TOUTENCOURT, in an orchard ankle deep in mud owing to the heavy rain which continued during the whole of the 29th. The camping ground was requisitioned and the Hut left in a very dirty condition. A number were received during the afternoon, but was cancelled later. On June 29th a formation was made of a Regimental School of Instruction for N.C.O.s & men qualifying for promotion, and for newly appointed N.C.O.s. Capt. Murray was appointed Commandant, and C.S.M Russell, Sergt Roberts & Sergt Simm comprised the Staff. This 'School' was arranged to operate wherever is rest billets, & is in elaboration of a similar system of training N.C.Os which was initiated at PLOEGSTEERT, & which was the first attempt that had ever been remained in the Batt & for junior N.C.Os although provoking in the rudiments of their programme.	
"	30th		On the 30th of June the Battalion was still in Hutment at TOUTENCOURT, and orders were received for a move the same evening. The weather was still very inclement.	

R. L. Aspinall Lt. Col
11th Batt Cheshire Regt.

June 30th 1916.

75th Bde.
25th Div.

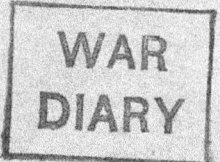

11th BATTALION

THE CHESHIRE REGIMENT.

JULY 1916

WAR DIARY or INTELLIGENCE SUMMARY

Army Form C. 2118

25/ July
11 Cheshire
Vol B

7.G.
O-4
16 sheets

Place	Date 1916	Hour	Summary of Events and Information	Remarks and references to Appendices
HEDAUVILLE	July 1st		On the night of June 30th/July 1st the Battalion marched from TOUTENCOURT to HEDAUVILLE, a distance of about 9 miles, getting into quarters at about 1.30 am and settling down into Huts & Tents. At 9.30 am a memorandum was received from the G.O.C. to the effect that offensive operations on a large scale, to which end the recent training has been directed, were to commence this day. All kits were stored in the village, and the Battalion was held in readiness to move at an hour's notice. During the night of July 1st/2nd orders were received for the Battalion at about 11.30 pm to hold itself in immediate readiness to move forward to AVELUY WOOD, but at 2.30 am the normal state of readiness was resumed. At 9.30 am on the morning of the 2nd but orders were received for the Battn to move up the remainder of the Brigade at 9.45 am to MARTINSART WOOD. The move was accomplished without difficulty – 2nd Lt R L Attwell DSO being in command of the Brigade in the march – the Brigadier General having proceeded to THIEPVAL for a reconnaissance of the trenches there. The Battn bivouaced along the ride in Martinsart Wood from W 4 d 2.3 to W 4 d 8.0 (Key Map 57 D S.E. 1/10,000) × Infantry. Officers per Company were sent to report to the H.Q. of the Batt: occupying the front of the Pendant Trenches in R 31 c × R 31 C (Map 57 D S.E. 1/20,000)	

AJESTY'S SE
FASTEN Envelope
OPEN by cutting
(E 3877)

ON HIS M
NATIONAL ECONOMY.
(6424) Wt. 25891/168 3,000,000 9/18 McA & W Ltd.

WAR DIARY
or
INTELLIGENCE SUMMARY
(Erase heading not required.)

Army Form C. 2118

Place	Date	Hour	Summary of Events and Information	Remarks and references to Appendices

The C.O. of the Batt: was admitted to Batt: Hd. at the Brigade Head Quarters (temporarily situated at about W 2 d 9.4 (Map ref as before) The Batt: received orders to make efforts for the recovery of the ammunition & kits it was short of, enemy & other fate that arose to befall it. The Officers who had proceeded to the Heute returned reporting the Helpless that no guides had met them as Brigade had arranged and that the Batt down in the Heute was unable to give any information unless as to the cause of there not being any guides. The Captain Officer was therefore instructed At about 5 pm an order was received by the Batt from 75= Brigade Head Quarters to issue each man in the Batt: will 2 bombs (mills) and to escort all picks & shovels that could possibly be carried by the men of the Battalion was ordered to move to the attack. The order was carried out - each man in addition now everywhere will the order was probably carrying an extra 50 rounds S.A.A. During the delivery of the bombs before issue, an accident happened

WAR DIARY or INTELLIGENCE SUMMARY

Army Form C. 2118

Place	Date	Hour	Summary of Events and Information	Remarks and references to Appendices

which resulted in the wounding of 3 men. After a period of uneven-
about 9.30 p.m. all Hostilities of the Brigade were commenced to the temporary Brigade
Head Quarters address at the obliteration of the Brigade began and very heavy orders
were made. These were later to the effect that the 75th Brigade was to attack a
section of hostile trenches just South of THIEPVAL. The 11th CHESHIRE were there in
the Right, 2nd S Lancs Regt on the Left; 8th Borders Regt in the Centre with the
8th S Lancs Regt in Brigade Reserve. The boundaries of the attack were
very largely stated and the hour of the attack was not issued in orders were to
be sent to units later, meanwhile units were to proceed at once, then assembly
positions in the trenches hereafter and await orders.
It was a significant fact that the C.O. required ORB attacked about 11 p.m. and
half attached to O.C. Coys. McKenzie to had glimpsed at Brigade
Head Quarters during the day. The attack was to be carried out in depth,
1st Battalion attacking in 8 waves - D Coy on the Right, McKey on the Right
C Coy in support of D & A Coys will B Coy held in Battalion Reserve.
The Battalion was fallen in and marched via BLACK HORSE Bridge

Army Form C. 2118

WAR DIARY or INTELLIGENCE SUMMARY
(Erase heading not required.)

Place	Date	Hour	Summary of Events and Information	Remarks and references to Appendices

to the Trenches taken over by R 31 a + c. Quarters of the 15th H.L.I. at entrance of the new covered the delay of BLACK HORSE bridge and conducted them into the Bedert trenches. At BLACK HORSE BRIDGE the situation was delayed as all the parties coming over had to use a single known as Communication trench – owing to a great number of wounded being brought down. During the delay the enemy shelled the vicinity of BLACK HORSE Bridge very heavily. The fully lit reconnaissance revealed by the enemy wireless Battalion was used by troops going up enemy's illuminating shells was very well illustrated. The great fun. It delayed the parties which was very disheartening to the parties. I reconnected the MTB station, advanced warship the avenue, recently it permitted the Batt to swing into the trenches without any output or disturbance from the enemy. Kept a patrol to proceed a mile ahead of Communication trench and have had about turn and relieved stretcher bearers wounded etc got out thirdly it recovered thousands of casualties from still fire — on the enemy never ceased to shell the trenches while the operation resulted forward about 2.15 am on the morning of the 3rd when the Battalion Head Quarters were established at CAMPBELL POST guarded by CAMPBELL AVENUE

WAR DIARY or INTELLIGENCE SUMMARY

Army Form C. 2118

Place	Date	Hour	Summary of Events and Information	Remarks and references to Appendices
THIEPVAL	3/7/16		(note dugout at O 36 d Map 57^D SE 1/20,000) immediately visiting the Companies the Adjutant found that considerable casualties had occurred during entrance the recently captured trenches. The British trenches were devoid of British troops and that the guide that the British trenches had no instructions other than to lead the entrance to some particular spot in the trenches that How much of the trenches each Company was to occupy was left to the imagination — in fact relief troops in fact had taken place. By about 5.30 am the Companies had more or less taken up some position. The trenches were exceedingly badly knocked about, with one another. The trenches were exceedingly badly knocked about, affording little cover from fire and in a great many places little cover from view. Steps were taken to organise the Bombers and to ascertain where the dumps were to ensure a supply of bombs and S.A.A. to the Companies. At about 6.20 a.m.	

The Dorset Regt. on the left & the 1/13th Cheshires (attached to the left battalion had been made) attacked the Geysenefontein Hill whose extent was not known. The right flank being exposed, the leading Companies of the Cheshire were immediately attacked and their ammunition reserves passed and Regt. NO MANS LAND in together. Word of this effect was immediately sent to the Commanding Officer who at once proceeded to the scene of action. The remaining troops meanwhile came under a withering fire from Machine Guns which at about 50 + yards from the first German line was absolutely untraversable. Line after line of the troops were mown down. The Commanding Officer was wounded with the reserve Company, was unfortunately killed and Captain Hill, who attempted, on then the Senior and J.M. Battalion devolved decided to get the men still living back into the trench from which they jumped off and to hold it as a defensive line. The remainder of the day was spent in trench warfare and carrying in of wounded and other casualties. Unfortunately the list of casualties was very large

Place	Date	Hour	Summary of Events and Information	Remarks and references to Appendices
THIEPVAL	1/7/16		and methodically every Company Commander. 20 Officers 657 Other Ranks entered the trenches and of these number 6 Officers 350 OR came out on the night of the 4th instant. On the 4th night the 3rd Ly/ the Battalion was ordered to STAFFAST TYNDRUM St moved further North and held another portion of front line up March with the 8th Border Regt – NA Keen of 10th Cheshire being filled by the 12th Wiltshire Regt. During the night 3-4th the rest of the Battalion who heavily shelled. Battle of Somme 9th these relief by the Cheshires were relieved by the 2nd Wiltshire Regt and proceeded to some assembly trenches in IVELYN WOOD. Arriver B Evans of the 2nd S. Somerset Regt together commanded of the Battalion the 5th instant and at 2 pm on the 5th the Battalion Arrived	
ALBERT	5/7/16		at ALBERT. The Battalion was billetted in ALBERT. On arrival W2 ?? ?? O. Major Evans and the O.C. Coys immediately made KEVSN HAMLEY out made a reconnaissance of the trenches in and around KEVSN HAMLEY A REDOUBT	

Army Form C. 2118

WAR DIARY or INTELLIGENCE SUMMARY

(Erase heading not required.)

Place	Date	Hour	Summary of Events and Information	Remarks and references to Appendices
ALBERT	6/7/16		At about 10.55 p.m. orders were received for the Batt to move at once & take up quarters at USNA REDOUBT. The Battalion moved off at 11.15 p.m. and after an extremely suffering evacuation & Albert & CR from Shrapnel and arrived after the heavier rain – There is not recorded night was spent in dugout in rain.	
-do-	7/7/16		At 4 pm orders were received to attack and consolidate the German 3rd & 4th lines stretching from X8d 80 to X8d 34 and X9c 55 to X6d 60 respectively. A Coy under the command of 2/Lt Cameron and B Coy under the command of Lt G E Martin were detailed at 6pm with instructions to reconnoitre the ground between Round hands and push out patrols along the German 2nd line the new Portland through the O— 1st I in the ALBERT-BAPAUME Rd and the track running from 57 D SE 1/20,000 the BOISELLE of the word OVILLERS-LA-BOISELLE on map M 630 & the C.O having entered boundaries of the Objective. followed the above 2 Companies with the rem^d^r of the Battalion and left it at the original British front line on the ALBERT BAPAUME Rd.	

WAR DIARY or INTELLIGENCE SUMMARY

Army Form C. 2118

Place	Date	Hour	Summary of Events and Information	Remarks and references to Appendices

whose cover was taken from considerable hostile shelling & Machine Gun Fire. The C.O. proceeded forward to gain touch with the B Companies, C & D Companies being left under the Adjutant with orders to follow at 2.30 pm. This was done but on passing the Head Quarters of the 8th S Lanc Regt A & B Companies were encountered, no action having been taken by these Companies with respect to the attack and the C.O. learnt of the C.O. being unknown Enquiry showed that the 2 leading Companies had then and the C.O. of the 8th S. Lanc Regt. reported that the head from X.14.6.9.0.6. was X.8.d.3.4. was occupied by the enemy. This head was according to the orders of the attack sufficed late in Brutal hands and completely covered the left of attack so that its capture was imperative from both objectives that had been laid down. The Adjutant proceeded at once to the Brigade Head Qrs on the subject & meanwhile alleged at once proceeded to the Head Quarters of 8th S. Lanc Regt to arrange with the C.O. of that Regt a combined turning action for the capture of the head X.14.6.9.0.6 & X.8.d.3.4. so that the real attack could be undertaken. Unfortunately this could not be arranged and the hours of darkness

Place	Date	Hour	Summary of Events and Information	Remarks and references to Appendices
OVILLERS 8/7/16			which were necessary for the success of the operations were then postponed for any action to be taken. Meanwhile an exceptionally heavy barrage fire had been struck with a piece of Sheffield and was temporarily interrupted but resumed the Battalion intelligence duty at 9 am, & reported that meanwhile the walls had been repelled by the G.O.C. 75th that overnight Remouille who immediately ordered Capt Hill to take 2 Companies to the Brigade, who immediately ordered Capt Hill to take 2 Companies to the trenches occupied by the 8th Staffs Regt, and send 2 Companies to the trenches near USNA REDOUBT. The remainder of 8th Staffs Regt, No 2 Company of the 11th Cheshire Regt, then in the forward trenches, the 75th Stoke Mortar Battery & the 75th M.G. Coy were then placed under the command of CAPT Hill who had orders to attack and capture the German 3rd & 4th lines from X.8.d.2.8 to X.8.d.8.0 and X.8.c.6 to X.9c.4.5. The orders for the attack were outlooked to Brigade Head Quarters and approved and the attack was timed to commence at midnight. The success of the whole operation depended on a surprise attack by 1 Company on the left & right of the first objective, the intelligence	

WAR DIARY or INTELLIGENCE SUMMARY

Army Form C. 2118

Place	Date	Hour	Summary of Events and Information	Remarks and references to Appendices
OVILLERS	9/7/16		having noticed that all trenches fulls right & S.E. of the objective were heavily manned and that the objective trenches were but lightly manned. Both these facts proved to be wrong but all the preliminary arrangements of the attack worked well. The Company reached the Right Flank of the objective without discovery and the attack commenced. The objective proved very difficult to take - Own attack by the 3rd S. Lancs. Regt. on the Pommiers Redt. having failed - and but success seemed assured as the first objective was entered by bombing parties in 3 places. The attack were not pushed with sufficient vigour for success and the troops retired having failed to take the objective. There seems no doubt that the troops were at that time too tired for the efforts demanded of them, having had little sleep but considerable work for many days. On the following day a bombing attack was again attempted about 12 noon but was unsuccessful. It should be noted that in reality these attacks had been preceded	

WAR DIARY
or
INTELLIGENCE SUMMARY
(Erase heading not required.)

Army Form C. 2118

Place	Date	Hour	Summary of Events and Information	Remarks and references to Appendices
OVILLERS	10/7/16 11/7/16		to our artillery preparation, but the wind was blown the necessarily the operation held up by the enemy and by the number of Machine Guns he had at his disposal. The day and the succeeding one was marked by an intense hostile bombardment and marked activity from snipers. One of the Lewis Gunning is victim also of Battalion Headquarters. The Brigade signalling officer fell to the sniper.	
"	11/7/16		On the night of the 11/12 the Battalion was relieved by the 8th Berks Regt and returned to the trenches in the neighbourhood of OVILLERS REDOUBT.	
"	12/7/16 13/7/16		These days were marked by the great number of fatigues and carrying parties that the Battalion supplied to and from the front line trenches. In the evening of the 13th Major W.K. Evanns D.S.O. the Manchester Regt took over Command of the Battalion. There are several points worthy of notice in the fighting of the passed few days. viz - the wonderful spirit shown by all ranks of the Battalion. Tired and weary the men never failed to respond to	

any certain demands of them. The casualties had been heavy and only 2 of the original officers of the Battalion remained viz Capt. C.F. Hills the Adjutant and Lt. H.D. Kay the signalling officer. Of the 11 new officers who joined the Battalion on July 1st - one 2/Lt. Hamilton took part in the action at THIEPVAL. On the night of the 3rd the officers returned to the trenches after being in NO MANS LAND for 14 hours and fought gallantly with the B attalion throughout the remaining 2 days. It is a fact that the B attalion continued the fighting until the 8th inst. It will therefore be seen that the work of the Battalion at OVILLERS was highly creditable. Few operations, e.g. beam gunners, bombers, etc. advanced after the action at THIEPVAL, the Battalion was led by subalterns & officers without any experience of trench warfare in active service conditions and the objectives attacked were not only some of the strongest positions of the enemy but were also held by some of his best troops, against whom the attacks were attacked without any preliminary preparation by artillery

WAR DIARY or INTELLIGENCE SUMMARY

Army Form C. 2118

Place	Date	Hour	Summary of Events and Information	Remarks and references to Appendices
OVILLERS	14/7/16		On the night 13/14th the battalion was ordered to take up a position on the German front & second lines as a reserve to the brigade, whose headquarters were moved from USNA REDOUBT to a more convenient place in the original German front line at LA BOISELLE. On the evening of the 14th/15th the battalion received orders to take a line of trenches to the N. of OVILLERS CHURCH — starting from a front consolidated by the 8th & 9th S. Staffs. — & bodies the night before. The battalion was ordered not to advance until the brigade on our right had succeeded in taking a line of trenches to protect our right flank. The battalion reduced in strength to about 100 available rifles was in position at the appointed hour, in spite of the late hour at which operation orders were received, C & D Coys lay out when the brigade on our right had reached their first objective. Day out that the brigade on our right had reached their first objective, but no word came from the right brigade who evidently still [fire] but no word came from the right brigade who had not reached their first objective. At dawn when breaking the battalion filed back into the trenches and returned to the LA BOISELLE — OVILLERS line feeling very annoyed that it had been unable to go forward to take a line which all were convinced would have been easily made good if our right had advanced with us. During the day however by a coup de main the 8th & 9th S. Staffs Regiment where work throughout had been	

1875 Wt. W593/826 1,000,000 4/15 J.B.C. & A. A.D.S.S./Forms/C. 2118.

WAR DIARY or INTELLIGENCE SUMMARY

Army Form C. 2118

Place	Date	Hour	Summary of Events and Information	Remarks and references to Appendices
AVILUERS	15/7/16		Of particular value manifest to edge most of the line where the brigade on our right should have taken the night before and consolidated this line into characteristic trench. Unfortunately Colonel Brassey of the 8th S-shires was killed just at the front. The same night the whole brigade was relieved by two battalions of another brigade and returned to a bivouac at SENLIS.	
	16/7/16		The brigade moved to another bivouac at HEDAUVILLE. Night wet, which added considerably to our discomfort.	
	17/7/16		The brigade moved again to ATIPIER, where it was understood we were to refit and train. Unfortunately a draft of 67 bantams had been added to the very elementary trained + no marching capacity pulled up fourteen of the battalion at SENLIS and trained and moral of the rest of the men at the expense of their inspection, and having been the battalion after two or three inspections, and having been formed by the divisional general that we should return to action after refitting, we marched to VAUCHELLES + mar! day to ACHEUX.	
	24/7/16 25/7/16		From ACHEUX on the afternoon of the 24th we relieved the 12th BDE in the line opposite BEAUMONT-HAMEL, two battalions holding the front line, one in support + one in reserve. This line was very quiet during our first four or six days. A trench termed "HUNTER-TRENCH" dug about 200 yards in front of our present front line and daily damaged by shell + trench mortars of the BOSCH who takes a particular	

1875 Wt. W593/826 1,000,000 4/15 J.B.C. & A. A.D.S.S./Forms/C. 2118.

WAR DIARY or INTELLIGENCE SUMMARY

Army Form C. 2118

Place	Date	Hour	Summary of Events and Information	Remarks and references to Appendices
MAILLY-MAILLET	31		alight in scattered shells all over NO MANS LAND during the night. The trench we took over was badly knocked about, in places was a great improvement on the THIEPVAL ditches or the BOSCH lines at OVILLERS and should assist the battalion to find its legs again. On the night 29/30th the working party in the SUNKEN ROAD or HUNTERS TRENCH was badly cut up by trench mortars and shells, which had registered on the trench during the day. The regiment was relieved by the 8th Borders Regt on the afternoon of the 30th July and retired to DIV RESERVE at near MAILLY-MAILLET. The day was spent in organisation of the Battalion, took over C.F.H. and providing working parties in the Stockade Cheefy in the SUNKEN Road above mentioned	

W.R. Crawd. Major
Commanding
11th (S) Batt. Cheshire Regt

"A" Form.
MESSAGES AND SIGNALS.
Army Form C. 2121.

TO	Head Quarters 75 Brigade

Sender's Number.	Day of Month.	In reply to Number.	
DE26	4	BM0675	AAA

Most of the losses were suffered 25 to 30 yards from enemy first line trench. Most of our troops did not get any nearer the enemy trench. A few small parties entered the enemy trench but have not been seen or heard of since. The wounds were chiefly on the left side of the stomach and on the head, and were inflicted by several MG's which were firing from a N.E.ly direction. One little gun was certainly also firing from the enemy first trench and seemed to be of greater speed (more resembling the Lewis) than the usual German MG.

A party of one Company lost their direction and moved off too much to the Right or South

"A" Form.
MESSAGES AND SIGNALS.
Army Form C. 2121.

and entered that part of the enemy trench at present held by the 15th H.L.I. A few rifles and [?] personnel were amongst the party. Nothing is known of Lt. Martin [?] personnel which were ordered to assist the Battalion. Not known if [?] & personnel were present. AAA

From: 11th Cheshire
Time: 11 a.m.

75th Brigade.
25th Division.

1/11th BATTALION

CHESHIRE REGIMENT

AUGUST 1916

Army Form C. 2118

WAR DIARY or INTELLIGENCE SUMMARY
(Erase heading not required.)

Instructions regarding War Diaries and Intelligence Summaries are contained in F.S. Regs., Part II. and the Staff Manual respectively. Title Pages will be prepared in manuscript.

Place	Date	Hour	Summary of Events and Information	Remarks and references to Appendices
Mailly Maillet	1/8/16 to 2/8/16		The Battalion still in Divisional Reserve, providing working parties in the trenches and being trained as far as possible under the existing circumstances.	
— do —	3/8/16 to 5/8/16		— do —	
			In the afternoon of the 5th the Battalion relieved the 2nd Border Regt in the AUCHONVILLERS sector being the help Battalion of the Brigade.	Shell
			Nothing of importance to report. The ordinary trench routine was carried on but great progress was made in the building of a new trench guide E of the Southern Road in O 4 d (Sheet 57 D SE 1/20,000)	
— do —	6/8/16 to 10/8/16		On the night of the 10th the Battalion was relieved by the 1st Coldstream Guards and proceeded to huttments in the BOIS DE WARNIMONT near AUTHIE (Sheet 57 D 1/40,000 I. 17.)	J. B. 5 sheets

1875 Wt. W593/826 1,000,000 4/15 J.B.C. & A. A.D.S.S./Forms/C. 2118.

WAR DIARY
or
INTELLIGENCE SUMMARY

Army Form C. 2118

Place	Date	Hour	Summary of Events and Information	Remarks and references to Appendices
BOIS-du-WARNIMONT	11/9/16 – 15/9/16		This period was spent in training, and was a very pleasant one. Company football matches, concerts were all indulged in. The Pierrots worked strenuously hard and fitted up a boxing ring, the scene of many excellent contests at dinner tables & Officers' Mess and every man had a comic tale to attend. On the 13th Major W.K. Greenan joined for duty, and on the 15th the Battalion moved to billets at RAINCHEVAL.	
RAIN-CHEVAL			On the following day Major G.A. Hawkins (late 11th Hussars) went sick and the draft of Bantams were sent away from the Unit to join the 15th Battalion.	
FORCEVILLE	17/9/16 – 18/9/16		The Battalion moved billets to FORCEVILLE. Lecture by Major Campbell to Bay'net Fighting & all Officers and NCOs.	
	19/9/16		The Brigade Major gave a lecture to all Officers on the organisation of working parties, and on the same day the Battalion moved to HEDAUVILLE where two 2 Coys were went into billets.	

and 2 Companies into HUTMENTS - the Officers being accommodated in tents. Thus the Battalion once more visited & the billage it stayed in on the eventful July 1st. During its stay stay at HEDAUVILLE every endeavour was made to freshen the training but also the time allowed for this was very necessary work was all too short and on the 22 of the Battalion relieved 16:7 border Regt in trenches in AUFLUY WOOD. The Hoytl ell all the remaining original 11st Batt. men flew back to July 2 1 but the two Battalions AUFLUY were destined to be ill greated duration.

A very happy time was passed in these trenches and little 26 walaut and except for the nightly working parties which had to be found for digging a new trench in NO MANS MIND in front TUIEPVAL and the shining of the ------, from which every me suffered very considerably the time

WAR DIARY
or
INTELLIGENCE SUMMARY

Place	Date	Hour	Summary of Events and Information	Remarks and references to Appendices
AVELUY WOOD			characterised by brilliant weather and we have a veritable holiday. The guns around were very quiet - to perhaps to damp its own as, but to those who had stayed, the noises 1 July 1 - 7 they caused little annoyance. On the 22nd the Battalion was relieved by the 1/5th KOYLI Regt and received 2 Coys moved to HUTHUILLE WOOD - two remaining in AVELUY.	
AUTHUILLE WOOD	22/8/16		On the 23rd A & D Coys moved from AVELUY WOOD to the BLUFF near BLACK HORSE BRIDGE (W6 Sheet 57D S.E. (?60,000)). Then man moved to the end of the newly dug new trench. A portion of the new British front line from R31 d.7.6 to R31 d.7.4 had to be garrisoned - a no man's land - so the trench was no more than series of steep holes which had its formation altered every day by the german shelling	

WAR DIARY or INTELLIGENCE SUMMARY

Army Form C. 2118

The Germans. The fatigue and working parties too were entirely wanting - all the front and alarm the men who had the test. Few trenches had to be dug and stores had to be carried. During frosts it all in the parties in the partial advance. The weather was unkind and added greatly to the descent. If the men went on making attempts work half difficult. Under these conditions men became hard had down brown boots though 2 feet of water, had to get the mud from a shovel and all under a heavy shelling which daily shattered the trenches dug. The two Jeanvillen had again received but again of the shelling and the endurance of the 11th Cheshire were not wanting.

W.R. Scoresby
Commd 11th Cheshire R/S

75th. INFANTRY BDE.

25th. DIVISION

11th. CHESHIRE REGT.

SEPTEMBER 1916.

"A" Form.
MESSAGES AND SIGNALS.

Army Form C.2121 (in pads of 100).

TO: 75th Infantry Brigade

Sender's Number.	Day of Month.	In reply to Number.	AAA
ADJ 612	31		

Herewith WAR DIARY in accordance with instructions contained in B.R.O. 157 d/- 23/10/16.

H.M. Hitchinson 2/Lt. a/Adjt.
for Lieut Colonel
Commanding 11th Cheshire Regt.

From: 11th Cheshires
Place:
Time: 6.0 p—

WAR DIARY or INTELLIGENCE SUMMARY

Army Form C. 2118

75/25

XI Cheshire Regt

Vol 10

9.G.
6 sheets

Place	Date	Hour	Summary of Events and Information	Remarks and references to Appendices
AUTHUILLE	1/9/16	HQ	The Battalion was in AUTHUILLE WOOD and Companies were distributed as follows:— 'C' Co. in the FRONT LINE (HINDENBURG Trench. R31c7.6 – R31d6.4) having relieved B Co; just the 10th Cheshire Regt in Support. A, B, & D Coys at the BLUFF (W6.c.2.8). The latter 3 Coys were allowed to rest in preparation for the attack on the morning of September 3rd	
do—	2/9/16		A & D Coys having been detailed to take part in the attack planned for the 3rd the officers of these two Companies reconnoitred the starting off positions in HINDENBURG Trench and examined the ground in front of the objective as far as possible. In the afternoon B Co. relieved C Co of the 10th Cheshire Regt. at Quarry Head Overton — Battalion Head Quarters moved from the AUTHUILLE WOOD and Battalion Head Quarters Post in QUARRY POST about 7 pm. Battalion was heavily shelled by the Germans but no casualties were sustained.	

WAR DIARY or INTELLIGENCE SUMMARY

Army Form C. 2118

Place: AUTHUILLE
Date: 3/9/16

The C.O. lectured the NCO's of A & D Coys on the plan of attack in the following morning and was very much struck with their eagerness and offensive spirit against the enemy.

The attack was timed to commence at 5.10am and was partly a general offensive operation along the whole British line in the active zone. A & D Coys were detailed to occupy the 8th Border Regt. in attacking and capturing a 2nd line of trenches after the first line had been captured by the 1st Wiltshire Regt. About 11.15pm orders were received informing the Batln. that the 8th Border Regt. and the 2 Coys of the Battalion in support of the 3rd Bde Regt. and the 1st Wiltshire Regt. failed, the attack by the 1st Wiltshire Regt. had failed; was cancelled.

B Coy were moved forward in support of C Coy the holding the front line; A Coy were moved to WOOD POST vacated by B Coy and D Coy were sent in support of the 5th S. Lancs Regt.

Army Form C. 2118

WAR DIARY
or
INTELLIGENCE SUMMARY
(Erase heading not required.)

Instructions regarding War Diaries and Intelligence Summaries are contained in F.S. Regs., Part II. and the Staff Manual respectively. Title Pages will be prepared in manuscript.

Place	Date	Hour	Summary of Events and Information	Remarks and references to Appendices
AUTHUILLE WOOD	4/9/16		At Westernside of the salient - LEIPZIG SALIENT. Later in the day an order was received whereby D Coy were moved to WOOD POST and A Coy were pushed forward to fill the gap in consequence of "Q" to the original German FRONT LINE. Between 6 am and 8 am A Coy relieved C Coy in FRONT LINE. C Coy returning to the trench vacated by A Coy. The front line which consisted mainly of a series of shell holes was in a very unhealthy state but much good work was done by the Coy in digging and revetting a trench. In the afternoon Pte No 16 & 3 Sgt George Marsden and 13259 Pte Patrick Moore both A Coy informed a very brave act by bringing in a wounded Corporal Notts Wiltshire Regt from NO MAN'S LAND in daylight.	
do -	6/9/16		D Coy at WOOD POST and A Coy in the FRONT LINE exchanged places. The past 3 days had been marked by nothing	

WAR DIARY
or
INTELLIGENCE SUMMARY
(Erase heading not required.)

Army Form C. 2118

Place	Date	Hour	Summary of Events and Information	Remarks and references to Appendices
-do-	7/9/16		Of importance except that no many casualties were sustained from the firing of our own batteries on firm there of the enemy. It thought 4th 6th & 7th the artillery fell into enemy active and considerable machine gun and rifle fire were exchanged both the enemy. Two patrols sent out by D Coy to my front took one of their dancering and counting a ditch held by German bombers.	
	8/9/16		In the morning the 7th Bn Battalion, after relief by the 8th Duke of Wellington (West Riding Regt) moved to BOUZAINCOURT which was receiving a few shells from the enemy and after a night's rest moved on the following day to Beauvillers.	
	9/9/16		This day was spent at ACHEUX. Obtained at ACHEUX. The Battalion moved to HAMPLIER.	

Army Form C. 2118

WAR DIARY
or
INTELLIGENCE SUMMARY
(Erase heading not required.)

Place	Date	Hour	Summary of Events and Information	Remarks and references to Appendices
			A glance at the list of Casualties on this date proved that once 21/8/16 the following had been sustained by the Battalion:- 3 Officers & O.R. killed; 1 Officer & 82 O.R. Wounded; 2 O.R. missing	
	11/9/16		The Battn. moved to AUTHIEUX	
AKENVILLE	11/9/16		The Battn. moved to AGENVILLE, and remained in billets in the village until the 25th inst. All the time was spent in training, of which games and competitions formed a considerable part. The weather was not however too favourable and greatly hindered the progress of training. Ranges, trenching huts, bayonet fighting galleries etc. were all constructed and gas & the like were advanced. Training was short however, orders were suddenly received by which the Battn. was once more to proceed to the scene of active operations in the vicinity of THIEPVAL.	

WAR DIARY
or
INTELLIGENCE SUMMARY
(Erase heading not required.)

Army Form C. 2118

Instructions regarding War Diaries and Intelligence Summaries are contained in F. S. Regs., Part II. and the Staff Manual respectively. Title Pages will be prepared in manuscript.

Place	Date	Hour	Summary of Events and Information	Remarks and references to Appendices
	23/9/16		The Batt. moved to Kryptic	
	24/9/16		The march was continued to LEFT A VILLERS where the Batt. remained until 29th inst. The few days spent here were noted for the enormous water keeps in "intensive digging".	
	29/9/16		The Bttn. marched to Bonyavenue and after spending a night in bivouacs moved the following day to CRUCIFIX CORNER at W.17 central (sheet 57D S.E. 1/40,000). He arrived were accommodated in dug outs. The remainder having shifted for themselves in bivouacs made from their mackintosh sheets.	

W.R. Townshend Lt.
Comnd 11th Cheshire Regt

75th Inf. Bde.
25th Division.

11th Battn.

CHESHIRE REGIMENT,

OCTOBER, 1916.

Army Form C. 2118

11th Ches. Reg.
75/25. Vol II

WAR DIARY
or
INTELLIGENCE SUMMARY
(Erase heading not required.)

Place	Date	Hour	Summary of Events and Information	Remarks and references to Appendices
AVELUY	1/X/16		In dug outs from W.17 b 70 to 75. Trench strength 17 Officers 590 O.R.	Ref. Map Sheet 57 D S.E. 1/20,000
"	3/X/16		280 men went in this morning on digging & carrying parties to MOUQUET FARM	
"	4.X.16		Relieved 49th Canadian Battn in Trenches, beginning at 6 P.M. 2Corp HESSIAN TRENCH R22 c95 to R21 d.99, joining with 8th Border Regt on E + 2nd S.Lancs Regt on W. 2 Corp in support in + behind ZOLLERN TRENCH EAST. Batt: H.Q. PICCADILLY, R28 c72.	
In trenches	5.X.1916		Owing to abominable weather conditions + flooded state of trenches + C.Ts. relief only completed 3:30 A.M.	
"	6.X.16		Coys in C.T. + Frtrench dug down + trenches deepened. Considerable shelling especially of C.T. Relieved in trenches by 11th Lancs Fusiliers, relief complete by 11.30 P.M.	
OVILLERS POST	7.X.1916		In dugouts at about W18 b.05 - 400 men had baths in AVELUY	
	8-9.X.16		Casualties during 48 hour duty in trenches 2 O.R. Killed + 14 O.R. wounded.	
	10.X.16	7 P.M.	Digging parties. Found digging party 180 strong to dig new BAINBRIDGE trench about R20 c85 - 2/Lt. F. E. Barton i/c covering party (5 wounded) by M.G. fire. Also 3 O.R. killed + 14 wounded.	
	11-12.X.16		Digging & carrying parties.	
	13.X.16	10 P.M.	Placed at tactical disposal of G.O.C. Y th Infy Bde.	
	14.X.16	8 P.M.	Batt: finished digging BAINBRIDGE trench	
Trenches	15.X.16		Moved 6 x 20.37 relieving 10th Cheshires. Brigade reserve. A + C Coys in Cheshire Trench, 74th Infy Bde. 1/2 Coy in HESSIAN TRENCH from R21 d.89 to R21 c.87. 1/2 Coy in support in ZOLLERN TRENCH WEST about R27 c.78.	
	16.X.16		A + C Coys relieved 11th Lancs Fusiliers, 74th Infy Bde. 1/2 Coy in HESSIAN TRENCH about R27 c.78. Digging parties - Digging harbor in ZOLLERN TRENCH WEST	10·G.

Army Form C. 2118

WAR DIARY
or
INTELLIGENCE SUMMARY
(Erase heading not required.)

Place	Date	Hour	Summary of Events and Information	Remarks and references to Appendices
Trenches	17/X/16		A & C. Coys relieved by 10th Cheshires & returned to X.2c.37 - Ration party to be picked & 2 wounded by a H.E. shell.	Ref. maps Sheet 57 D.S.E. 1/20,000
	18/X/16		Instruction of Battn in details of attack intended for tomorrow.	
	19/X/16		Relieved 10th Cheshires in HESSIAN TRENCH from R.22.c.37 to R.21.c.77 - Men filed in by Coys, one from each platoon consecutively so as to space them in trench. R.21.d.89 - Orders reached Battn H.Qs HESSIAN TRENCH for attack by 4 waves in Company column. Battn H.Qs HESSIAN TRENCH moved back to dug-out at X.20.c.37, about midday attack postponed 24 hours. A Coy French strength O-22 - O.R. 526 & C. Coy to R.27.B.17. 2/Lieut. HICKEY wounded. At 2 a.m. received orders for postponement of attack a further 24 hours. Message to A Coy did not reach them in time to prevent them moving up again to trench. Orders about 6.P.m that 8th Borders an Assault column on left(?) known as 11th Cheshires, or REGINA TRENCH from R.21.a.33 to R.21.b.62.55 A Coy 11th Cheshires & another officer and a selected N.C.O attached to 8th Borders by 8 a.m. Battn 4.0 moved back to R.27.5.17. A by N.C.Regiment held HESSIAN TRENCH vacated by B. 8th Br. Bn & Btn S.Lancs.	
	20/X/16			
	21/X/16		After the attack to reinforce garrison of REGINA trench. C. Coy were split up as carrying parties for 3 Batts delivering attack. D. Coy moved up also reinforced Borders after attack of REGINA trench. Battn two Somme bombs	

WAR DIARY
or
INTELLIGENCE SUMMARY
(Erase heading not required.)

Army Form C. 2118

Place	Date	Hour	Summary of Events and Information	Remarks and references to Appendices
Trenches	21/X/16 cont.		In the attack, A Coy captured a German Machine gun, cleared with a bombing party dug out in REGINA TRENCH, & went about 400 yards beyond along road, clearing several dugouts & taking prisoners. Casualties — 2/Lieut R.W.L. Scott - killed. 2/Lieuts A.G. Carpenter, C.F.S. Rhodes, H. Holland & K.P. Hall - wounded. 2/Lieut E.S. Lacy - missing. Other Ranks - 8 killed, 52 wounded, 14 missing.	Ref Map Sheet 57 D SE 1/20000
	22.X.1916		Relieved by 7pm by 19th Division, marched to camp near ALBERT (W20a)	
WARLOY AUTHIEULE	23.X.1916 24.X.1916		Marched to WARLOY - billets. Marched to huts at AUTHIEULE	
	25.X.1916 - 29.X.1916		The battalion was in huts at AUTHIEULE. The time was spent in cleaning up and refitting.	
	29.X.1916		The battalion marched to DOULLENS and entrained at 6.19 p.m. arriving at BAILLEUL about 1 a.m. 30th and thence marched to billets in and around METEREN.	
	31.X.1916		A certain number of baths were allotted at BAILLEUR, the remainder of the day was spent in training.	

W.R. Brown Lieut Colonel
Commanding VI(9) Batt. Cheshire Regt.

75th Inf. Bde.

25th Division

11th Battn.

CHESHIRE REGIMENT,

NOVEMBER, 1916.

WAR DIARY or INTELLIGENCE SUMMARY

Army Form C. 2118

XI Cheshire Regt
Vol 12

H.G.
2 sheets

Place	Date	Hour	Summary of Events and Information	Remarks and references to Appendices
METEREN	1/11/16		The Battalion marched from METEREN about 8.0 am and took over huts at DE SEULE uneventfully, then for one night.	
	2/11/16		On the following day the Battalion moved up and took over a portion of the line held by the 7th Division to the North of PLOEGSTEERT WOOD the left of the Battalion resting on the River DOUVE. The distribution of companies being 1 Company in the Front line, 1 with some in hand in support, 6 Platoons in the SUBSIDIARY LINE and the 4th Company in Battalion Reserve at STAFFORD HOUSE. The garrisons of the trenches were occupied throughout the time in clearing and generally improving the trenches. The company in reserve found parties daily for carrying rations and R.E. Stores to the other companies. After 3 days the company in the front line was relieved by the company in reserve. The battalion was relieved by the 8th Border Regt and returned to billets and dugouts in the RED LODGE area, Batt. H.Q and one company remaining in their original position at STAFFORD HOUSE. After the first day in rest when the battalion had baths, working parties were found daily for work on the trenches. About 130 men were found daily for these parties.	
	14/11/16		The battalion again relieved the 8th Border Regt in the line. Work was carried on daily in the trenches as before.	
	20/11/16		The battalion was relieved by the 8th Border Regt having been in the RED LODGE area and returned to the billets	

Army Form C. 2118

WAR DIARY
or
INTELLIGENCE SUMMARY
(Erase heading not required.)

Place	Date	Hour	Summary of Events and Information	Remarks and references to Appendices
	21/11/16		The period is not one of much interest. On the first day the batn. had baths and the remainder of the time was spent in finding working parties for work in the front line and communication trenches. The battalion relieved the 9th Border Regt. in the line took over carrier as usual.	
	26/11/16		Total casualties during the month 2 O.R. wounded 2 O.R. wounded (still at duty)	

A R Sandwick Lt Col
Comm 11th Cheshire Regt

75th Inf. Bde.

25th Division

11th Battn.

CHESHIRE REGIMENT,

DECEMBER, 1916.

WAR DIARY or INTELLIGENCE SUMMARY

XI Cheshire Rgt

Nov /15

12. P.
5 sheets

Place	Date	Hour	Summary of Events and Information	Remarks and references to Appendices
	1/12/15		The Battalion was relieved by the 8th Border Regt and returned to dugouts in the RED LODGE area. The afternoon & two days and the morning of the 2nd were spent by the battalion in fitting the this day was spent in cleaning up and inspection of arms & equipment. On the 4th the Battalion were handed over to the 7th Royal Irish Rifles of the 31st Division.	
	4/11/15		The battalion took over a new sector East of PLOEGSTEERT WOOD relieving the 9th Batt. Loyal North Lancs Regt of the 7th Brigade. This was the exact sector held by the battalion last year and is situated on the North by the STRAND and on the South by LONDON AVENUE. The dispositions in this sector were 3 Coys in the front line and immediate support and 1 Coy in the support line, Battalion H.Q. was established at RIFLE HOUSE. The Trenches in this sector consist almost entirely of breastworks and work had to be constantly carried on in pumping and draining the trenches and in building up and revetting the breast works and parapet in places where they had fallen in	

WAR DIARY or INTELLIGENCE SUMMARY

Place	Date	Hour	Summary of Events and Information	Remarks and references to Appendices
	19/12/16		The battalion was relieved by the 8th Border Regt and moved into support. 1 Coy holding the line of fire immediately behind the work held by the 8th Border Regt. 1 Coy situated at TOUQUET BERTHE FARM and 2 Coys at PLOEGSTEERT HALL. Battalion H.Q. was established at PRESTON FARM. During this period all available men with the exception of the garrisons of the huts were sent daily to work for the Pins battalion holding the line.	
	16/12/16		The battalion relieved the 8th Border Regt in the line. Work was again carried on in drawing and improving the trenches.	
	25/12/16		On it was intended to carry out a raid upon the German trenches upon December 25th in the neighbourhood of the LE GHEER road a raiding party consisting of Major HARGREAVES 2/Lieut KNOWLES 2/Lieut WRIGHT and 50 O.R. was withdrawn from the trenches and sent down to the camp of a Tunnelling Company of Canadian R.E. about 1 mile East of BAILLEUL on the BAILLEUL-ARMENTIERES road where daily practices were carried out till the raid taken for the raid. Daily was now volunteers and suffered no casualties	

WAR DIARY
or
INTELLIGENCE SUMMARY

(Erase heading not required.)

Army Form C. 2118

Instructions regarding War Diaries and Intelligence Summaries are contained in F. S. Regs., Part II. and the Staff Manual respectively. Title Pages will be prepared in manuscript.

Place	Date	Hour	Summary of Events and Information	Remarks and references to Appendices
			25th However the Germans were found to be holding in their own front of the road as the northern attack was being delivered. A raiding party consisting of 3 Officers and 28 OR which gave a very efficient covering artillery barrage shot at about 8.30 a.m. encountered an enemy to enemy to a point about 80 yds south of the road. A [illegible] difficulty was experienced in getting through the enemy wire and the party could not to seen by our patrols to party on which shell could not be seen by our patrols to party on casualty was Scott's rand at the head. On his return he found [illegible] and it [illegible] were killed. Easy one [illegible] captured and our barrage exploded of the bombs by enemy from the trenches made in the enemy trenches could be easily seen and not find any traces of the four numbered. All did from hostile to carry out the northern attack was brought up have been taken as evidence of German arms in a wiring company in front of the country parts. No one [illegible] was numbered at	

1875 Wt. W593/826 1,000,000 4/15 J.B.C. & A.   A.D.S.S./Forms/C. 2118.

WAR DIARY or INTELLIGENCE SUMMARY

Army Form C. 2118

Place	Date	Hour	Summary of Events and Information	Remarks and references to Appendices
	23/9/16		the form a raiding party have been the offer of that actually required. The Battalion was relieved by the 8th Berks Regt. and moved into reserve at LE ROMARIN. The following day men spent in bathing and a certain amount of training was carried out during the period. A draft of 93 O.R. joined on the 24th. On the 25th a fine performance was given at the Brigade Cinema Theatre to the Battalion and on the 26th a dismounted event was held and on the 27th a performance was given by the Divisional Pierrot troupe. The semi-final and final of the football competition started in September at AGWELLE was complete and won by the final being won by "A" Coy	
	28/9/16		A successful raid was carried out on the German trenches in the neighbourhood of the LE GHEER road. It had actually been intended to enter the German lines in two places north and the other south of the road and a separate party had been detailed to enter at each place. On the night of the	

WAR DIARY or INTELLIGENCE SUMMARY

Army Form C. 2118

Place	Date	Hour	Summary of Events and Information	Remarks and references to Appendices
	26/4/16		distance south and south of the point of entry to club from the north. Heavy rain in the enemy trenches. It is almost certain that three Germans became casualties. Our raiding party returned to our trenches after about 28 minutes. Total casualties 1 O.R. killed, 6 O.R. slightly wounded. The battalion again relieved the 8th B.W. Rgt. in the line. During the two particular situations was had to the improvement of the wire along the whole of the battalion front. The casualties during the present month have been: 3 killed, 13 wounded, - Missing. The present strength of the battalion is 24 officers, 445 O.R.	

W.R. [signed] Lieut. Col.
Commdg: 11(S) Bn Cheshire Regt.

WAR DIARY
or
INTELLIGENCE SUMMARY
(Erase heading not required.)

Army Form C. 2118

1/1 Cheshire Regt.

Place	Date	Hour	Summary of Events and Information	Remarks and references to Appendices
PLOEGSTEERT	1/1/17		The Battalion were in the line on the East of PLOEGSTEERT WOOD	
	2/1/17		The 75th Brigade was withdrawn from the line and went back for a fortnight training. The sector held by the 75th Brigade was partly taken over by the 74th Brigade on the left and partly by the 7th Brigade on the right. The battalion was relieved by the 7th Loyal North Lancashire Regt and proceeded after relief to billets in NIEPPE.	
NIEPPE	3/1/17 to 16/1/17		The first days in the training area was spent in cleaning up. Later on subsequent days a strenuous programme of training was carried out. Particular attention was paid to the practice of the attack which was carried out first by companies then by the battalion and finally by the whole brigade over a flagged course	
LE TOUQUET	17/1/17		The 75th Brigade relieved the 7th Brigade in the line. The battalion relieved the 3rd Worcester Regt. on the extreme South of the Divisional sector.) The battalion boundaries were defined by the river LYS on the South and ESSEX CENTRAL FARM on the North. The dispositions in the area were 3 Companies in the front and immediate support line and 1 Company in reserve at TANCREZ COTTAGES (SHEET 36 N.W. C.8.d.80.55) Battalion Headquarters were established at SURREY FARM. The sector taken over was found to be very wet and also the parapets	

WAR DIARY or INTELLIGENCE SUMMARY

Place	Date	Hour	Summary of Events and Information	Remarks and references to Appendices
	22/1/17		subjected to bombardment by enemy M.M. Trench mortars.) This necessitated a great deal of work being done in clearing the existing drains and in digging others.	
LE BIZET	23/1/17		The enemy bombarded the sheds of the battalion subways from 2.0 pm till 5.30 p.m. causing considerable damage to one trench. 3 O.R. were killed by the bombardment and 3 wounded. The battalion was relieved by the 8th Border Regt.	
			at LE BIZET.) Two companies were employed as to the permanent garrison of the front in the brigade area while the other two companies formed working parties for the battalions in the line. Owing to the hard frost very little work with the exception of wiring could be done.	
LE TOUQUET	29/1/17		The battalion relieved the 8th Border Regt. in the line. The frost still held and the result was that the only work that could be carried on was wiring. Casualties during the month 3 O.R. killed 10 O.R. wounded Trench strength on the 31st. 18 Officers 519 O.R.	

R. Guinness Major
Commanding 11th Cheshire Regiment.

"A" Form.
MESSAGES AND SIGNALS.

Army Form C.2121
(in pads of 100).

TO: 75th Infantry Brigade.

Sender's Number: M.C. 877
Day of Month: 1
AAA

Herewith WAR DIARY of the
Battalion for the month of
February 1917.

A.K. Evans
Lieut. Colonel
Commanding 13 Cheshire Regt.

WAR DIARY
or
INTELLIGENCE SUMMARY

Army Form C. 2118

11 Cheshire Regt

Place	Date	Hour	Summary of Events and Information	Remarks and references to Appendices
LE TOUQUET	1/2/17		The battalion was in the line in the LE TOUQUET sector. The front still held and little or no work with the exception of wiring could be done. At 6.0 p.m. on this date the enemy attempted to raid the GAP between the left of the battalion sector and the sector held by the 2nd South Lancashire Regt. He was quickly driven out by our barrage and Lewis Gun fire and evidence of enemy casualties was found next morning.	
PONT DE NIEPPE	4/2/17		The battalion was relieved by the 8th Border Regt and moved to billets in PONT DE NIEPPE	
LE BIZET	8/2/17		The battalion moved into support at LE BIZET.	
LE TOUQUET	10/2/17		The battalion relieved the 8th Border Regt in the line. Towards the end of this tour the frost began to break rendering the condition of the trenches very bad.	
	14/2/17	3.0am	The enemy placed a heavy Trench Mortar Barrage on a small portion of our line near MONMOUTH HOUSE and under cover of this succeeded in entering our trench. They did not remain more than 5 minutes but succeeded in capturing 3 men of a post which was isolated by the Box Barrage. During this tour our casualties were exceptionally heavy for the sector amounting to about 24.	
LE BIZET	16/2/17		The battalion was relieved by the 8th Border Regt and moved into support at LE BIZET. Co the thaw was now continuing rapidly the battalion was fully occupied with working parties in the trenches.	
	19/2/17		Major the Hon. W. E. Guinness left the battalion to take up the appointment of Brigade Major to the 74th Brigade. Captain R Hallinan (CHESHIRE REGT.) joined the	

WAR DIARY or INTELLIGENCE SUMMARY

Army Form C. 2118

Place	Date	Hour	Summary of Events and Information	Remarks and references to Appendices
LE TOUQUET	24/2/17		Battalion as 2nd in Command. The battalion relieved the 8th Border Regt: in the line.	
NIEPPE	25/2/17		The Brigade was relieved by the 1st NEW ZEALAND Brigade the Battalion being relieved by the 2nd WELLINGTON REGT: after relief the battalion moved into billets at NIEPPE.	
GODEWAERS-VELDE	26/2/17		The battalion marched to billets at GODEWAERSVELDE via BAILLEUL, METEREN and FLETRE. On this day a draft of 87 O.R. joined the battalion. The following day was spent in cleaning up, & on the 28th the programme of training was begun. Casualties during the month 10 O.R. killed, 4 O.R. missing, 2/Lt: HUGHES and 19 O.R. wounded. (two of whom since died of wounds). Trench Strength on the last day of the month 26 Officers 581 O.R.	

1/3/17.

W R Evans Lieut: Colonel
Commanding, 11 CHESHIRE REGT

Army Form C. 2118

11 Cheshire Copy 1

Vol 16

15A
2nd

WAR DIARY
or
INTELLIGENCE SUMMARY
(Erase heading not required.)

Instructions regarding War Diaries and Intelligence Summaries are contained in F. S. Regs., Part II. and the Staff Manual respectively. Title Pages will be prepared in manuscript.

Place	Date	Hour	Summary of Events and Information	Remarks and references to Appendices
GODENAERS-VELDE	1/3/17		The battalion remained in billets at GODENAERSVELDE until March 13th having carried out during the period considered many of battalion schemes	
RENESCURE	13/3/17		On the 13th the battalion marched to RENESCURE via ST SYLVESTRE CAPPEL and HAZEBROUCK a distance of about 14 miles, and on the 14th the march was continued via ARQUES, WIZERNES, LUMBRES and ACQUIN to the WESTBECOURT area a distance of about 15 miles. The billets occupied by the battalion were my centrand Battalion Headquarters and one company were at WESTBECOURT two companies at VAL D'ACQUIN and another form th at BOUVELINGHEM.	
WEST BE-COURT	14/3/17			
ETREHEM	20/3/17		On the 20th of March the 25th Division began to move forward again the battalion moving on this date to billets in the village of ETREHEM and LEULINGHEM a distance of about 6 miles. On the following day the	
SERCUS	21/3/17		battalion marched to SERCUS via WISQUES WIZERNES ARQUES and RENESCURE. On this day a draft of 57 of the Reserve Batt. joined the battalion	
GRAND SEC BOIS	22/3/17		On the 22nd the battalion marched to the BORRE area when it was billetted in and around the hamlet of GRAND SEC BOIS	

Army Form C. 2118

WAR DIARY
or
INTELLIGENCE SUMMARY
(Erase heading not required.)

Instructions regarding War Diaries and Intelligence Summaries are contained in F. S. Regs., Part II. and the Staff Manual respectively. Title Pages will be prepared in manuscript.

Place	Date	Hour	Summary of Events and Information	Remarks and references to Appendices
BUTTERSTEENE	24/3/17		On the 24th the battalion marched to the BUTTERSTEENE area and was billeted in large farms to the South of the village. On this date a draft of 20 from the Shropshire Light Infantry joined the battalion.	
	1/4/17		Fighting Strength at the end of the month 31 Officers 722 O.R.	

Lieut. Colonel
Commanding 12 Cheshire Regt.

Army Form C. 2118.

WAR DIARY 11th Cheshire Reg
INTELLIGENCE SUMMARY.
(Erase heading not required.)

Vol 17

Place	Date	Hour	Summary of Events and Information	Remarks and references to Appendices
OUTTERSTEENE	1-4-17		In billets at OUTTERSTEENE where Battalion training was continued.	
NEUVE EGLISE	4-4-17		The Brigade took over a sector of trenches to the East of WULVERGHEM on a sur-Battalion front on the 5th. The Battalion moved on the 4th in the Reserve at BULFORD CAMP (hut about one mile S. of NEUVE EGLISE). The burying of cable between NEUVE EGLISE and WULVERGHEM was taken over from the 11TH LANCASHIRE FUSILIERS (74th Brigade) and very available man in the Battalion was occupied in this work every night. This work was extremely difficult owing to the wet nature of the ground and the lucency of the church to fall in before the necessary depth of 8 feet had been attained. This unimportant work however was very satisfactory performed and the Battalion was congratulated by the Divisional Commander.	
STEENWERCK	13-4-17		On the 13th the Battalion was relieved by the 7th Brigade, and moved into billets in the STEENJE area, the Battalion being located in farms about one mile WEST of STEENWERCK. In this area the Battalion found large day parties for the construction of ammunition dumps and other work in the back area. On the 17th the working parties were taken over by the 8TH BORDER REGT, and the remaining time in this area was spent by the Battalion in training.	16 G. 3 sheets

A6945 Wt.W11424/M1160 350,000 12/16 D. D. & L. Forms/C./2118/14

WAR DIARY
or
INTELLIGENCE SUMMARY.
(Erase heading not required.)

Army Form C. 2118.

Place	Date	Hour	Summary of Events and Information	Remarks and references to Appendices
LE BIZET.	20/4/17		On the 20th the Brigade took over the LE TOUQUET sector with one Battalion in the line. The Battalion moved into support, two companies finding the garrisons of the supporting points, and two companies being in LE BIZET.	
LE TOUQUET	25/4/17		On the 25th the Battalion relieved the 2ND SOUTH LANCASHIRE REGIMENT in the line. The front extending from the RIVER LYS on the South to LOWNDES AVENUE (on the South edge of PLOEGSTEERT WOOD) on the North, a distance of 1300 yards, and consisted of the fronts held by two Battalions of the 75th Brigade from January 15th to February 25th 1917. At 12.30 a.m. on the 28th, cloud gas was discharged from one of the GAPS in the Battalion front and at the same time gas projectors were fired from the right company frontage into FREIINGHIEN. The enemy retaliation was very slight and only six casualties (all slight wounds) were sustained by the Battalion. Patrols which were sent out to investigate the effects of the gas were unable to get through the enemy wire. It is thought however, that the projection of gas met with good results as the enemy were not seen or heard in the town during the following 24 hours. It is believed that this method of projecting gas bombs had previously	

Army Form C. 2118.

WAR DIARY
or
INTELLIGENCE SUMMARY.
(Erase heading not required.)

Instructions regarding War Diaries and Intelligence Summaries are contained in F. S. Regs., Part II. and the Staff Manual respectively. Title pages will be prepared in manuscript.

Place	Date	Hour	Summary of Events and Information	Remarks and references to Appendices
			been used on one occasion only.	
ERQUINGHEM	29/4/17		On the night of the 29th/30th the Battalion was relieved by the 36th AUSTRALIAN BATTALION and moved to Billets in the RUE DORMOIRE about one mile west of ERQUINGHEM on the BAC ST MAUR road arriving in billets about 4 am.	
OUTTERSTEENE	30/4/17		At about 2 pm on the 30th the Battalion marched to the same billets at OUTTERSTEENE which it had left on the 4th of the month.	
			Fighting Strength 1-4-1917 = 32 Officers 737 Other Ranks	
			" " 30-4-1917 = 35 " 739 "	
			Casualties. 1 Killed	
			11 Wounded (2 of whom Died of wounds).	

W.R. Swans
Lieut. Col.
Comdg. 11th (S) Batt Cheshire Regt.

WAR DIARY
INTELLIGENCE SUMMARY

Army Form C. 2118.

XI Cheshire R

Vol 18

17 GR
3 sheet

Place	Date	Hour	Summary of Events and Information	Remarks and references to Appendices
OUTTERSTEENE	1.5.17		The Battalion remained in billets at OUTTERSTEENE until the 5th. While in this area the finals of the Brigade inter-Company Football was played which was won by D Company. On the previous day the Battalion won the Brigade Two County Cup.	
ST MARIE CAPPEL	8.5.17		The Battalion marched to ST MARIE CAPPEL via STRAZEELE and CAESTRE for a Musketry Course and Range Practice at the Divisional Musketry School.	
LA CRECHE	15.5.17		On the 15th the Battalion marched via CAESTRE and BAILLEUL to BLOUWERS at LA CRECHE. During the first week in this area the whole Battalion was engaged on important work on the neighbouring dumps, the latter being mainly the unloading of ammunition from trains. During the second week the Battalion was relieved of this work for three or four days, which were spent in practising the attack over a flagged course on MONT DE LILLE (about one mile East of BAILLEUL).	
RAVELSBURG	24.5.17		The Battalion marched to Camp in a field at S.17.a (Map France Sheet 28) Working parties of between two and three hundred were found daily for work on dumps and battery positions.	
	31.5.17		The Battalion GS Lieut Sty. the Battalion to march to VIEUX BERQUIN on this	

Army Form C. 2118.

WAR DIARY
or
INTELLIGENCE SUMMARY.
(Erase heading not required.)

Instructions regarding War Diaries and Intelligence Summaries are contained in F. S. Regs. Part II and the Staff Manual respectively. Title pages will be prepared in manuscript.

Place	Date	Hour	Summary of Events and Information	Remarks and references to Appendices
camp at MORBECQUE			Strength on 1st May 1917. 39 Offr. 851 O.R. Strength on 31st May. 41 Offr. 922 O.R. Drafts joining during month. 3 Offr. 106 O.R. Education B.O.R. obtained.	

W.R. Evans
Lieut Col.,
Commdg. 11th (S) Border Regt.

War Diary

of

11ᵀᴴ (S) BATTALION CHESHIRE RGT.

For the Month of June 1917.

Army Form C. 2118.

WAR DIARY
INTELLIGENCE SUMMARY.
(Erase heading not required.)

Instructions regarding War Diaries and Intelligence Summaries are contained in F. S. Regs., Part II. and the Staff Manual respectively. Title pages will be prepared in manuscript.

Place	Date	Hour	Summary of Events and Information	Remarks and references to Appendices
			REFERENCE MAP SHEET 28.	
RAVELSBURG	1.6.17		The Battalion was in Camp at RAVELSBURG where working parties were found for unloading ammunition and work on the various dumps.	
NEUVE EGLISE – DRANOUTRE road	3.6.17		At about 10 p.m. on the 3rd the Battalion marched to PIONEER CAMP just EAST of the NEUVE EGLISE – DRANOUTRE road (Sheet 28 T.2.C.) In this days on the 4th and 5th about 450 men were found by the Battalion to work under the 130th Field Company R.E. The work consists mainly of the improvement of the assembly trenches and the overland tracks just behind our front line and consequently was almost entirely night work.	
			Attack on Messines – Wytschaete ridge	
			At 3.10 a.m. on the 7th June the 25th Division in conjunction with divisions on the right and left carried out an attack on the MESSINES – WYTSCHAETE RIDGE. The 75th Brigade was in Divisional Reserve and the task allotted to the Battalion was to advance from a line to be captured by the 8th South Lancashire Regt running from LUMM FARM (O.26.Z.1.8.) to O.33.a.5.6. and establish a line of strong points between farm at O.27 central and the BLAUWE POORTBEEK SOUTH of DESPAGNE FARM (O.33.b.5.8.)	
			The Battalion moved off from PIONEER CAMP at about 10 p.m. and was in position in the assembly trench (DURHAM TRENCH) by 1 a.m. while assembling and before ZERO	

Army Form C. 2118.

WAR DIARY
of
INTELLIGENCE SUMMARY.
(Erase heading not required.)

Instructions regarding War Diaries and Intelligence Summaries are contained in F. S. Regs., Part II. and the Staff Manual respectively. Title pages will be prepared in manuscript.

Place	Date	Hour	Summary of Events and Information	Remarks and references to Appendices
			the battalion was shelled with lachrymatory shells which caused a few casualties. From ZERO onwards very few casualties were caused by enemy retaliation. Two Officers were wounded in the Assembly Trench.	
		6.45 am	the battalion moved forward. On reaching the top of the MESSINES-WYTSCHAETE RIDGE casualties were caused by machine guns from LUMM FARM and the vicinity on the left flank of the Battalion where the enemy were still holding out. During the advance from the BLACK LINE (O.26.a.1.8 - O.33.a.5.6) many prisoners, four field guns and one machine gun captured. By 9 a.m. the objective was reached and owing to the non-arrival of the Battalion on the left the farm at O.27. was still holding out and consolidation commenced. Between 11 a.m. and 12 Noon the enemy were seen massing in O.34.B and O.35.a. and between 1 pm and 2 pm a counter attack was launched from that direction. About 600 of the enemy attacked in four waves but were met by our Lewis guns and rifle fire and were finally dispersed by our S.O.S. barrage leaving a large number of dead. At 3.10 pm the 52nd Battalion A.I.F. passed through the Battalion to capture a further objective. This Battalion apparently went too far NORTH and thus a gap was left in front of our right post. This	

A6945 Wt. W14422/M1160 350,000 12/16 D. D. & L. Forms/C./2118/14.

Army Form C. 2118.

WAR DIARY
or
INTELLIGENCE SUMMARY.
(Erase heading not required.)

Instructions regarding War Diaries and Intelligence Summaries are contained in F. S. Regs., Part II. and the Staff Manual respectively. Title pages will be prepared in manuscript.

Place	Date	Hour	Summary of Events and Information	Remarks and references to Appendices
	8/6/17.		was confirmed by the fact that between 5pm and 6pm about 60 of the enemy were seen approaching this post but were driven back by Lewis Gun and rifle fire. The night passed fairly quietly and consolidation proceeded rapidly. During the 8th the enemy shelled the line of posts also the vicinity of Battalion Head Quarters O.27.c. The shelling was exceptionally heavy at times and at 6pm a heavy bombardment was opened on the right and on the line of posts held by the Battalion. The enemy did not attack on the Battalion front and by 8pm all was quiet. At 8.30 pm. the enemy again opened a very heavy bombardment on our outpost and all communication was severed inopposite. Some Aucklands who had retired through our post reported that the enemy was attacking and that our line of posts had fallen. By 11 p.m. however, communication was restored and the line of posts was found to be intact.	
NEUVE EGLISE	9/6/17.		Between 1 a.m. and 4 a.m. the Battalion was relieved by the 8th Battalion Loyal North Lancashire Regt. and moved back to camp at NEUVE EGLISE. Total casualties 5 officers 160 other ranks.	
	11.6.17		The Battalion "B" team rejoined from MORBECQUE.	

Army Form C. 2118.

WAR DIARY
or
INTELLIGENCE SUMMARY

(Erase heading not required.)

Instructions regarding War Diaries and Intelligence Summaries are contained in F. S. Regs., Part II. and the Staff Manual respectively. Title pages will be prepared in manuscript.

Place	Date	Hour	Summary of Events and Information	Remarks and references to Appendices
TRENCHES E. of MESSINES	12.6.17		On the night of the 12th/13th the Battalion relieved the 13th Bn N.I.F. in the front lines, the Battalion sector consisting of our TRENCH from O.34.d.1.8 to MUNS WALK U.4.d.4.7. with two advanced posts 200 yards near of the road running through GAPAARD. the 8th Border Regiment being on the left and the 8th South Lancashire Regt on the right. The Battalion was subjected to intermittent shelling for about 12 hours and about 7.30 p.m. on the 13th the front line was heavily bombarded causing several casualties. During the night and the morning of the 14th a new trench was dug by the Battalion from O.34.d.15.55 to U.4.b.40.85	
	14/6/17		At 7.30 p.m. under cover of our artillery barrage the 8th Border Regt and 8th South Lancashire Regiment advanced and established themselves on a line of chong pouts on the line DECONINCK FARM (O.34.b.7.7) - GAPAARD - LES QUATRE ROIS CABARET (O.35.c.8.4) - STEIGNAST FARM (U.5.a.2.7). During this operation our companies (with the exception of one which remained to hold the Battalion frontage from which the 8th Border Regt advanced) were withdrawn to the neighbourhood of Battalion Headquarters U.3.b.1.8. Offrs and three wire companies carried up R.E. material to the chong pouts line and started to	

Army Form C. 2118.

WAR DIARY
or
INTELLIGENCE SUMMARY.
(Erase heading not required.)

Instructions regarding War Diaries and Intelligence Summaries are contained in F. S. Regs., Part II. and the Staff Manual respectively. Title pages will be prepared in manuscript.

Place	Date	Hour	Summary of Events and Information	Remarks and references to Appendices
			was it. The enemy retaliation to our barrage was fairly heavy and the situation was not quite settled about 11 p.m.	
	15/6/17		On the night of the 15th the strong points were taken over from the 6th Border Regiment by three Companies of the Battalion, the 4th Company remaining in its original position in OWL TRENCH.) Battalion Also Quartis also moved to OWL TRENCH. The last two days in this sector were considerably quieter and very few casualties were caused. Total casualties 2 Officers 49 other ranks.	
PIONEER CAMP	17.6.17		On the night of the 17th the Battalion was relieved by the 11th Lancashire Fusiliers and returned to PIONEER CAMP. In this camp the time was spent in cleaning up and generally refitting. On the 23rd the Battalion started to march to the Bony area by a series of night marches. On the night of the 23rd/24th the Battalion marched to SEC BOIS via	
SEC BOIS	24/6/17		BAILLEUL – STRAZEELE – STRAZEELE STATION. On the night of the 24th/25th the march was continued to the MERVILLE area via VIEUX BERQUIN and NEUF BERQUIN. On the	
MERVILLE	25/6/17		night of 25/26 the Battalion marched via ST HILAIRE and on the night 26th/27th the	
ST. HILAIRE	26/6/17		following night the battalion reached its destination marching through WEST RE HEM – FEBVIN PALFART – FLECHIN – BOMY	

WAR DIARY
or
INTELLIGENCE SUMMARY.
(Erase heading not required.)

Instructions regarding War Diaries and Intelligence Summaries are contained in F. S. Regs., Part II. and the Staff Manual respectively. Title pages will be prepared in manuscript.

Place	Date	Hour	Summary of Events and Information
RECLINGHEM	27.6.17		to RECLINGHEM. The 28th was devoted to cleaning up and on the 29th training was started.
			Awards gained in the attack on Messines Ridge.
			BAR TO D.S.O. Lieut. Col. W. K. EVANS, D.S.O
			MILITARY CROSS. Capt. & Adjutant W. H. McKERROW; Chaplain R. LeB. NICHOLSON, W. A WILLIAMS.
			2nd Lieutenants L. F. CLIST, C. WRIGHT.
			D. C. M. Acy. Sgt. Major C. LOUTH - Sgt. FLETCHER - Lance Corporal SMASH.
			MILITARY MEDALS. 21.
			Casualties: KILLED. 2nd Lieut. C.F.S. RHODES. 32. O.R.
			D. O. W. 2nd Lieuts C. POTTS, E. R THOMAS. 11. O R
			WOUNDED. Capt. J A KNOWLES, M.C. - 2nd Lieuts. S.C. STEVENS, F. LATHAM, B. MOLYNEUX,
			P.R. DIGBY, T.C. MORGAN, H.M. BALLANCE, R PAUL
			178. O. R.
			MISSING. 5. OR.
			Strength at beginning of Month. 41 Officers 920 OR.
			" " end " " 32 " 718 "
			Reinforcements received 1 " 26 "
					W Nicholson Major
					Lt. Lieut. Col.
					Comg. 11th (S) Bn Cheshire Regt

11 Cheshire Regt
No C 26
75/25

Army Form C. 2118.

WAR DIARY
or
INTELLIGENCE SUMMARY.
(Erase heading not required.)

Instructions regarding War Diaries and Intelligence Summaries are contained in F. S. Regs., Part II. and the Staff Manual respectively. Title pages will be prepared in manuscript.

Place	Date	Hour	Summary of Events and Information	Remarks and references to Appendices
RACLINGHEM	1.7.17		Ref maps Sheet 28 France: Sheet 27 France Belgium 5A	
			The Battalion was in billets at RACLINGHEM where Company and Battalion training was continued.	
THIENNES	27.7.17		The Battalion moved by bus to STEENBEQUE and marched from thence to billets at THIENNES.	
DOMINION CAMP	29.7.17		On the following day the move was continued by bus via HAZEBROUCK and ABEELE to a point about 1 mile S.W. of POPERINGHE where the Battalion left the buses and marched to DOMINION CAMP (Sheet 28 H 25. B. 6). In the area large working and carrying parties were found for work in the vicinity of ZILLEBEKE LAKE while a party of 100 men were contiguously increased to 150 working purposively under the 171st Tunnelling Company, R.E. by whom they were rationed and accommodated.	
CAMP AT SHEET 27. L.17.d.9.6.	22.7.17		On the night of the 22nd the Battalion marched to Camp at Sheet 27. L.17.d.9.6. where Battalion training was carried out.	19B sheet
	30.7.17		The Battalion marched to its assembly position (Sheet 28 H.21. B 2.6) arriving about 3 am on the 31st. At 7.20 a.m. the Battalion moved forward to its position of readiness in the vicinity of RAILWAY WOOD Sheet 28 I.11.D.6.4 where it remained the rest of the day.	
	31.7.17			

STRENGTH ON LAST DAY OF MONTH   34 Officers   951 O.R.

CASUALTIES DURING MONTH   KILLED 1 Off. 6 O.R.
                          WOUNDED 1 Off. 19 O.R. (includes 1 Or. D.O.W.)
                          MISSING   1 O.R.

DRAFTS JOINING DURING MONTH   2 Off.   184 O.R.

M Hoare
Major for Lt Col
Commg 11th Bn Cheshire Regt

for Lieut Col Comm 11/Bn Cheshire Regt

Army Form C. 2118.

WAR DIARY
or
INTELLIGENCE SUMMARY.
(Erase heading not required.)

11th Bn Cheshire Regt.

Vol 21

Instructions regarding War Diaries and Intelligence Summaries are contained in F. S. Regs., Part II. and the Staff Manual respectively. Title pages will be prepared in manuscript.

Place	Date	Hour	Summary of Events and Information	Remarks and references to Appendices
WESTHOEK RIDGE.	1/8/17		On the morning of the 1st about 7 a.m. the Battalion moved up from the position of readiness in RAILWAY WOOD and relieved the 2nd Batt. West Yorkshire Regt, who were holding the line on the WESTHOEK Ridge. During the whole of this tour the weather remained very bad and the trenches, where they existed, were knee deep in water. A large number of casualties were caused by enemy shell fire which was exceptionally heavy throughout the tour.	
YPRES.	6/8/17		On the night of the 5th/6th the Battalion was relieved by the 9th Royal North Lancashire Regt, (74th Brigade) and went into reserve in dugouts in the Esplanade, YPRES, with Headquarters at the LILLE GATE.	
	9/8/17		On the afternoon of the 9th, the Battalion was relieved by the 1st Wiltshire Regt, and moved back to HALIFAX CAMP (H.14.c.).	
HALIFAX CAMP. WESTHOEK RIDGE.	11/8/17		On the night 11th/12th, the Battalion again moved up to the WESTHOEK Ridge, relieving the 9th Royal North Lancashire Regt, who had advanced the line some 500 yards from the position held by the	

Army Form C. 2118.

WAR DIARY
or
INTELLIGENCE SUMMARY.

(Erase heading not required.)

Instructions regarding War Diaries and Intelligence Summaries are contained in F. S. Regs., Part II. and the Staff Manual respectively. Title pages will be prepared in manuscript.

Place	Date	Hour	Summary of Events and Information	Remarks and references to Appendices
	13/8/17		Battalion on the 5th inst: The enemy shell fire during this tour was again very heavy. On the night of the 13th, the Battalion was relieved by two battalions of the 8th Division, the 2nd. Rifle Brigade and the 2nd. Lincolnshire Regt.,	
DOMINION CAMP.			and moved to DOMINION CAMP.	
	16/8/17		On the 16th, the 8th Division made an attack and the 75th. Brigade was placed at their disposal. The Battalion marched in the afternoon	
YPRES.			to the ESPLANADE, YPRES and at night found a carrying party of 200 to carry up stores and rations for the 8th. Division.	
	17/8/17		On the evening of the 17th., the Battalion was relieved by the 18th. London Regt., marched to VLAMERTINGHE and was taken from there by bus to GODEWAERSVELDE, arriving early on the 18th.	
GODEWAERSVELDE.	18/8/17		The Battalion marched to billets in the STEENVOORDE Area, where they	
STEENVOORDE.	20/8/17		stayed for the remainder of the month and carried out battalion training.	
	29/8/17		On the 29th, the Brigade Horse Show and Sports were held and on	

Army Form C. 2118.

WAR DIARY
or
INTELLIGENCE SUMMARY.
(Erase heading not required.)

Place	Date	Hour	Summary of Events and Information	Remarks and references to Appendices
	30/9/17		and on the 30th the Brigade Boxing Tournament.	
			Strength at the beginning of month 34 Officers 951 Other Ranks	
			Drafts arriving during month 3 " 69 "	
			Casualties during month 10 " 136 "	
			Strength at end of month. 28 " 759 "	
			Captain R. Mallinson } Killed in Action 2nd Lt. H.P. Blair } Wounded in Action	
			2nd Lt. G.L. Martin } 2nd Lt. H.A. Lawson }	
			" G.H. Watson } Capt. J. Batson }	
			" J.E. Morgan } 2nd Lt. Carpenter }	
			" J.R. Dickinson } 2nd Lt. Tooke }	

W.R. Crans
Lieut. Col.,
Comdg. 11th (S) Cheshire Regt.

Army Form C. 2118.

WAR DIARY
or
INTELLIGENCE SUMMARY.
(Erase heading not required.)

Place	Date	Hour	Summary of Events and Information	Remarks and references to Appendices
STEENVOORDE	1.9.17.		On the morning of the 1st the Battalion marched to DOMINION CAMP (G.23.B. Sheet 28) via ABEELE	
DOMINION CAMP	2.9.17.		and RENINGHELST and on the following morning to a camp on the OUDERDOM - DICKEBUSCH road about a mile west of DICKEBUSCH. A few casualties were caused by bombs dropped from enemy aeroplanes during the night.	
DICKEBUSCH	3.9.17.		The Battalion remained in this camp for three days and on the 5th went to relieve	
HALFWAY HO:	5.9.17.		the 3rd Worcester Regt in support at HALFWAY HOUSE (I.17.a. Sheet 28) when working parties were found to bury cable and man tracks in the forward area. On	
DICKEBUSCH	9.9.17.		the morning of the 9th the Battalion was relieved by the 18th London Regt 47th Division and moved back to the camp previously occupied at DICKEBUSCH.	
HALIFAX CAMP	10.9.17.		On the morning of the 10th the Battalion marched back to HALIFAX CAMP (H.17.Sh.28) by 11h. The Battalion bivouacked in this camp on the night of the 10th by aeroplane bombs and shells from a high velocity gun and on the night of the 11th the Battalion bivouacked in the fields.	
CAESTRE	12.9.17.		On the afternoon of the 12th the Battalion moved by bus to camp at CAESTRE	
THIENNES	13.9.17.		and continued the move by march route on the 13th to THIENNES via HAZEBROUCK and STEENBECQUE.	

Army Form C. 2118.

WAR DIARY
~~INTELLIGENCE SUMMARY.~~
(Erase heading not required.)

Instructions regarding War Diaries and Intelligence Summaries are contained in F.S. Regs., Part II. and the Staff Manual respectively. Title pages will be prepared in manuscript.

Place	Date	Hour	Summary of Events and Information	Remarks and references to Appendices
ALLOUAGNE	14.9.17		On the 14th the Battalion marched to billets in ALLOUAGNE via AIRE – ST. HILAIRE and	
	25.9.17		LILLERS. These billets were occupied until the 27th, and company and Battalion training was carried out. Lieut Col. M. K. Evans D.S.O. left to take command of the 182nd Infantry Brigade after having commanded the Battalion for 14th months.	
	26.9.17		The Divisional Horse Show and Fete was held at Brigade Headquarters at ALLOUAGNE	
NOEUX LES MINES	27.9.17		The 75th Brigade moved forward to take over the line from the 71st Infantry Brigade. The Battalion moved on this day to NOEUX LES MINES on Division.	
CITE ST PIERRE	28.9.17		On the following night the Battalion relieved the 1st Leicestershire Regt in close support in CITE ST. PIERRE (Sheet 36ᶜ S.W.), the Brigade front from N.13.B.6.2.10 N.8.C.7.1. being held by the 8th South Lancashire Regiment.	
	29.9.17		Major L.W. Blackacre, 1st Royal Welsh Fusiliers Regt. took command of the Battalion.	

STRENGTH OF BATTALION	32 OFFS	771 OR
CASUALTIES. KILLED	-	15 "
WOUNDED	-	"
MISSING	3 "	66 "
REINFORCEMENTS		

C.W.Blackacre Major

Comdg. 11th (S) Batt. Cheshire Regt.

T2134. Wt. W708–776. 500000. 4/15. Sir J. C. & S.

WAR DIARY
or
INTELLIGENCE SUMMARY.

(Erase heading not required.)

Army Form C. 2118.

11th Q ?? Regt

Place	Date	Hour	Summary of Events and Information	Remarks and references to Appendices
			Reference Map:- LA BASSÉE, 1/10,000.	
CITÉ ST. PIERRE.	1:10:17		The battalion was in support in CITÉ ST. PIERRE where parties were found to work in the forward area.	
LES BREBIS	4:10:17		On the evening of the 4th the Brigade was relieved by the 6th Division who extended their front to the right to take over the front held by the 8th S. LANCS. The battalion moved that night to billets in LES BREBIS.	
VAUDRICOURT.	5:10:17		On the following day, the battalion marched through NOEUX LES MINES to billets in VAUDRICOURT and the neighbouring villages of VERQUIN and BROUVIN.	
Front Line 6:10:17 (Canal Sector)			On the 6th the battalion relieved the 2nd OXFORD + BUCKS L.I. (32nd Division) in the CANAL Sector from A.22.d.1.9. on the North to A.27. B.5.4. on the South. Disposition being — 3 Companies in the front line, 1 Company in support and Batt. H.Q. at BRADELL POINT, A.21.c.1.7. Transport lines at LE QUESNOY. The trenches taken over were in good condition but a large amount of work had to be done to prevent them becoming very bad in wet weather.	

Army Form C. 2118.

WAR DIARY
or
INTELLIGENCE SUMMARY.
(Erase heading not required.)

Instructions regarding War Diaries and Intelligence Summaries are contained in F. S. Regs., Part II. and the Staff Manual respectively. Title pages will be prepared in manuscript.

Place	Date	Hour	Summary of Events and Information	Remarks and references to Appendices
LE PRÉOL	12.10.17		The battalion was relieved on the night of the 12th by the 8th BORDER Regt. and moved into reserve billets at LE PRÉOL.	
Front line	18.10.17		On the 18th the battalion relieved the 8th BORDER Regt. in the front line. During this tour special attention was paid to the wire in the front, which in places was very weak.	
Support	24.10.17		On the 24th the battalion was relieved by the 8th BORDER Regt. and subsequently relieved the 8th S. LANCASHIRE Regt. in support. Disposition - 1 Company finding the garrison of the KEEPS on the Brigade front, 1 Company in support to each of the two battalions holding the front line, and the fourth Company at PONT FIXE, A.I.4.d.3.9. with Batt. H.Q. A.I.4.a.9.6. In this area parties totalling 350 men were found daily for work under the R.E. On the 30th the battalion again relieved the 8th BORDER Regt. in the front line.	
Front line	30.10.17			

WAR DIARY
or
INTELLIGENCE SUMMARY.

Army Form C. 2118.

(Erase heading not required.)

Place	Date	Hour	Summary of Events and Information	Remarks and references to Appendices
			Strength – Oct. 1. – O. O.R.	
			32 – 171.	
			31. 40 – 171.	
			Casualties during month:-	
			2/Lieut Arthur Searle. Killed in Action. 4. K/A.	
			" Thomas Pritchards. Died of Wounds. 1. D.O.W.	
			5. W.	
			Reinforcements during month:-	
			10. Officers 37. O.R.	
			CUSTEAURU Lieut. for	
			Comdg. 11th (S.) Bn. Cheshire Regiment	

Army Form C. 2118.

WAR DIARY
or
INTELLIGENCE SUMMARY.
(Erase heading not required.)

11th Bn. Cheshire Regt.

Vol 4

Instructions regarding War Diaries and Intelligence Summaries are contained in F. S. Regs., Part II. and the Staff Manual respectively. Title pages will be prepared in manuscript.

Place	Date	Hour	Summary of Events and Information	Remarks and references to Appendices
CANAL RIGHT SECTOR	1/11/17		11th (S) Battalion Cheshire Regiment holding the line from A.22.a.1.7. to A.27.b.7.6. - D company holding left sector. B company centre, A company on the right, and C company in support.	TRENCH MAP LA BASSEE 36a N.W.1. Ed. 9a 1/10000
LE PREOL	5/11/17		Battalion was relieved by 8th Batt. Border Regiment. Battalion in Brigade Reserve.	
			3rd - 8th. Polygon in line from A.22.a.1.7. to A.15.b.9.9.	
CANAL RIGHT SECTOR	11th-16th		The Battalion relieved the 8th Battalion Border Regt. and held same Battalion front. - MILLTRENCH and a part of THE LANE badly damaged by enemy medium mortars fired in retaliation for our 2" mortars on FRANKS KEEP.	
PONT FIXE	17th - 22nd		Battalion in support. The whole Battalion with the exception of the garrison of the Keep was occupied in working parties under the R.E. while in this area.	
CANAL RIGHT SECTOR	23rd-27th		Battalion relieved 8th Batt Border Regt. D Coy on left. B Coy in centre - A Coy on right and C Coy in support. From 1.30pm to 2.15pm 23/11/17 we bombarded FRANKS KEEP and RYANS KEEP with trench mortars. Polygon holding line overnight. Coys hospitals in AUCHY 25/11/17.	
BETHUNE	28th		Relieved by 7th Lancashire Fusiliers, 42nd Division. Left for Bethune where men were billeted in the ORPHANAGE.	
BAS RIEUX	29th		Left for BAS RIEUX (LILLERS) arriving at 1pm.	28 G 2 sheets

Army Form C. 2118.

WAR DIARY
or
INTELLIGENCE SUMMARY.
(Erase heading not required.)

Instructions regarding War Diaries and Intelligence Summaries are contained in F. S. Regs., Part II. and the Staff Manual respectively. Title pages will be prepared in manuscript.

Place	Date	Hour	Summary of Events and Information	Remarks and references to Appendices
LAIRES	30th		Left for LAIRES via LILLERS, ST HILAIRE, AUCHY-AUX-BOIS and CUHEM.	
			Strength at beginning of month 40 offrs. 773 O.R.	
			" " end " 38 " 769 "	
			Officers struck off strength Major J.F. Lomax (to command 13 R.W.F. 38th Div.)	
			2nd Lieut. Jn Newson (to England sick)	
			" M.N. Ruddick (" " ")	
			" L. Kitchingman (to 1st Bn Cheshire Regt)	
			" A.D. Munroe (" " ")	
			Draft received during month. 4 offrs. 3 O.R. (2nd Lt. Kitchingman, A. Munroe, Harper, E. Thomas.)	
			Casualties " " 1 " (2/Lt. Jones)	
			" " 4 "	

J.H.M. Cornah Major
Comdg 11th (S) Bn Cheshire Regt.

Army Form C. 2118.

WAR DIARY
INTELLIGENCE SUMMARY.

(Erase heading not required.)

11th Bn. Cheshire Regt.

Vol 25

Instructions regarding War Diaries and Intelligence Summaries are contained in F. S. Regs., Part II. and the Staff Manual respectively. Title pages will be prepared in manuscript.

Place	Date	Hour	Summary of Events and Information	Remarks and references to Appendices
	DECEMBER	REF. MAP. LENS. 11.		
LAIRES.	1st - 3rd		Training area for the 75th Brigade.	
	Night 3/4.		Marched from LAIRES to ANVIN and entrained for ACHIET LE GRAND via ABBEVILLE.	
	" 4/5.		Under canvas just outside GOMIECOURT.	
	5th		Marched to ROCQUIGNY via BAPAUME.	
ROCQUIGNY	5th - 9th		Battalion resting in huts.	
BAPAUME	9th - 16th		Under canvas on piece of ground 400 yards east of BAPAUME and just south of BAPAUME - CAMBRAI Road. Battalion provided working parties for burying cable south of VAULX-VRAUCOURT.	
	16th		Marched to FAVREUIL and took over two R.E. camps.	
FAVREUIL	16th - 21st		Battalion provided working parties for burying cable south of VAULX-VRAUCOURT.	
	21st		75th Infantry Brigade relieved 7th Infantry Brigade in line opposite QUEANT.	
	21st - 27th		Battalion in support around LAGNICOURT and NOREUIL.	
	27th		Battalion relieved 8th South Lancs. Regt. in the line.	
	27th - 31st		Holding front line.	

STRENGTH AT BEGINNING OF MONTH	= 38. OFFS.	768. OR.
" " END "	" 36. OFFS	733. OR.
CASUALTIES DURING MONTH	" - "	7. OR.
DRAFTS.	" - "	8. OR.

[signature] Lieut. Col.
Comdg 11th (S) Bn Cheshire Regiment

Army Form C. 2118.

WAR DIARY
or
INTELLIGENCE SUMMARY.
(Erase heading not required.)

11 Bn Graham Regt

VII 26

Place	Date	Hour	Summary of Events and Information	Remarks and references to Appendices
LAGNICOURT Trenches	1/1/1918		The Battalion was holding the line NORTH of LAGNICOURT.	
FAYREUIL	2/1/1918		On the night of the 2nd the Battalion was relieved by the 8th BATT. LOYAL NORTH LANCASHIRE REGT. 7th Brigade and moved to No. 13 Camp FAYREUIL.	
	4/1/1918		Christmas dinner for the men in the Divisional Theatre, FAYREUIL. During the remainder of the time spent at FAYREUIL a certain amount of training was carried out but this was much interfered with by working parties which were found for the erection of huts and the protection of Divisional Head Quarters.	
VAULX	14/1/1918		On the 14th the 75th Brigade relieved the 7th Brigade in the line, the Battalion relieving the 8th LOYAL NORTH LANCASHIRE REGT in reserve at VAULX. Two companies were found daily to work for the front line battalions in clearing the trenches which had fallen in owing to the sudden thaw. One company was employed on excavation at the new Brigade Head Quarters VAULX and the remaining company found parties for the R.E. at VAULX DUMP.	
LAGNICOURT Trenches	20/1/1918		On the night of the 20th the Battalion relieved the 7th SOUTH LANCASHIRE REGT in the same sector as before.	

Army Form C. 2118.

WAR DIARY
or
INTELLIGENCE SUMMARY.
(Erase heading not required.)

Place	Date	Hour	Summary of Events and Information	Remarks and references to Appendices
LAGNICOURT	20/1/18		The trenches were still in very bad condition and all companies were continually employed in clearing them.	
	21/1/18		On the 21st a barrel belt of wire was put out across the HIRONDELLE valley by a wiring party of the 7th Brigade for which a covering party of 70 men was found by the Battalion.	
			The day was actually quiet there being practically no shelling of the trench system.	
FAVREUIL	26/1/18		On the night of the 26th the Battalion was relieved by the 8th Batt. LOYAL NORTH LANCASHIRE REGT. and moved to 70/13 camp FAVREUIL.	
	27/1/18		From the 27th onwards 250 men were found daily to work on the TANKS — MORCHIES (Depot) line. Smaller parties were also found for erecting huts, work at R.E. DUMP etc., the whole working strength of the Battalion being employed daily.	
	31/1/18		Lieut. Col. to R.S. Prior. D.S.O., M.C. was granted a month's leave and Major G. Downes. M.C., Border Regiment attached Royal South Lancashire Regiment took command of the Battalion.	

WAR DIARY
or
INTELLIGENCE SUMMARY.

(Erase heading not required.)

Army Form C. 2118.

Place	Date	Hour	Summary of Events and Information	Remarks and references to Appendices
			Strength of Battalion as the beginning of the month. = 36 Off. 733 O.R.	
			" " " " end " = 38 " 785 "	
			Drafts received during month = *3 " 46 "	
			Casualties during month " 1 " 3 "	
			* Lieut. M. M. Barry	
			" C. A. Beard	
			2/Lt. R. H. Owen	
			[signature]	
			Major	
			Comdg. 11th (S.) Bn. Cheshire Regiment.	

WAR DIARY
or
INTELLIGENCE SUMMARY. 11 (S) Bn Cheshire Regt.

Army Form C. 2118.

(Erase heading not required.)

Vol 27

Place	Date	Hour	Summary of Events and Information	Remarks and references to Appendices
FAYREUIL	1.2.18		The Battalion was in billets at FAYREUIL finding 250 men daily for work on the YAULX - MORCHIES line in addition to small working parties in the vicinity of the camp.	
	6.2.18		Draft of 10 officers and 200 other ranks joined from the 13th Battalion CHESHIRE REGIMENT.	
LAGNICOURT	7.2.18		On the evening of the 7th the Battalion relieved the 10th Battalion CHESHIRE REGIMENT in the LAGNICOURT sector, the Battalion Boundaries and dispositions being the same as the previous tour. The enemy artillery was slightly more active than in the previous tour but only one casualty was sustained by the Battalion.	
FAYREUIL	12.2.18		On the night of the 12th the Battalion was relieved by the 2nd Battalion YORK and LANCASTER Regiment, 62nd Division, and moved back to No 11 Camp FAYREUIL	
LOG EAST WOOD	13.2.18		On the following day the Battalion marched to a Camp on the Western edge of LOG EAST WOOD via SAPIGNIES, BIHUCOURT and ACHIET LE GRAND	
	14.2.18		Major T. S. WILKINSON, 8th BORDER REGIMENT took over command of the Battalion from Major G. DARWELL, M.C.	
			The remainder of the month was spent in training the whole Division being in Corps Reserve in the vicinity of ACHIET LE PETIT. An average of 200 hours work was done per day for the first week and four hours per day for the remainder of the period.	

Army Form C. 2118.

WAR DIARY
or
INTELLIGENCE SUMMARY.
(Erase heading not required.)

Place	Date	Hour	Summary of Events and Information	Remarks and references to Appendices
			Particular attention was paid to Musketry and Range Practice. During the latter part of the month the afternoons were devoted to games and recreational training and Brigade football and boxing competitions were organised.	
			Strength on 1/2/1918. 37 Officers 784 O.R.	
			" " 28/2/1918. 46 " 990 O.R.	
			Casualties " " " 2 O.R.	
			Drafts joined during month 10 " 233 O.R.	
			Officers leaving during month:—	
			CAPT. R.J. CHOMELEY M.C. TO ENGLAND 6 months leave & duty	

			× { Captain CHOLMELEY. R.J. M.C.
			                   such { " COOLE. R.S.
			                          { " RYDEN. H.
			                          { " WOODLOCK. F.T.
			                          { " PIGOTT. D.F.
			                          { " HASSALL. J.T.
			                          { " JONES. W.R.
			                          { " POOLE. D.A.
			                          { Lieut. WILYMAN. T.
			                          { " HARVEY. F.W.	

J.J. Wilkinson Major.

Comdg 11th/13 Battalion Cheshire Regiment.

25th Division.
75th Infantry Brigade.

WAR DIARY

11th BATTALION

CHESHIRE REGIMENT

MARCH 1918

C.E.165

76th Infantry Brigade.

Herewith War Diary for
month of March 1918.

M. Wimperley

5/4/18.
c/o Adjt: for Lt: Col:
Cdg: 11 Cheshire Regt:

Army Form C. 2118.

WAR DIARY
or
INTELLIGENCE SUMMARY.
(Erase heading not required.)

11th Bn: Cheshire Regt.

Place	Date	Hour	Summary of Events and Information	Remarks and references to Appendices
LOGEAST CAMP.	1/3/18		The Battalion was in rest at LOGEAST CAMP from 1st to the 13th and continued the training. Several attentions were paid to Musketry and attack formations. On the night of the 7/8th an all night Brigade assembly and attack exercise was carried out.	
	7/3/18		Major G. DARNELL M.C. returned from leave and resumed command of the Battalion. Major T.S. WILKINSON returned to 8th Border Regt. on the 8th. On this date Major N.B. HAY-WILL M.C. relinquished the appointment of 2nd in Command on going to England for 6 months tour of duty. Major E.R.S. PRIOR D.S.O, M.C. became 2nd in Command on his return from leave on the 9th.	
	12/3/18		On the afternoon of the 12th the Brigade moved forward to what was believed the enemy might attack on the 13th. The Batt. was accommodated in BERKELEY CAMP, BIHUCOURT.	
BERKELEY CAMP. BIHUCOURT.	13/3/18		The Battalion stood to at 5. a.m. but no attack materialised. The Battalion remained at this camp until the morning of the 21st and the usual training was carried out.	

WAR DIARY or INTELLIGENCE SUMMARY

Army Form C. 2118.

No. 1.

SUMMARY OF OPERATIONS
21.3.18 — 28.3.18.

Place	Date	Hour	Summary of Events and Information	Remarks and references to Appendices
			By Major S.T.C.	
BERKELEY CAMP	21.3.18	5 am	Heavy enemy barrage was heard on the C.M.G.S. Front and Battalion turned ro.	
BIHUCOURT		6.30am	Orders received to move at 9.15am.	
R.14.c.5.3.		9.15am	Battalion moved off under Major E.F.S. Prior, D.S.O. P.S.C. (Strength 20 C's, 510 O.R.) and marched to No. 11. Camp FAVREUIL (B team, Stores etc were left at BERKELEY CAMP)	
No. 11. CAMP				
FAVREUIL		12 Noon	Battalion reached No. 11. Camp where the men had dinners. The camp was being shelled by H.V. Gun.	
H.14 Central		1.30pm	Battalion was placed in 6th Div. reserve and moved to a position N. of VAUX – BEURATRE road, H.14. Central, two Companies North and two South of the VAUX–BEURATRE road. The position was reached at about 2.30pm and about 2 hours afterwards the Battalion was placed at disposal of 16th Inf. Bde. and ordered to take up a position in the 6th Division and the 59th Division on the East side at about H.30.a.7.6. Major Prior went in advance to 16th I.B.H.Q. in VAUX for further instructions. As the Battalion was moving off to take up this position this order was cancelled	

A6945 Wt. W14422/M1160 350,000 12/16 D. D. & L. Forms/C/2118/14.

WAR DIARY or INTELLIGENCE SUMMARY

Army Form C. 2118.

No. 2.

Instructions regarding War Diaries and Intelligence Summaries are contained in F.S. Regs., Part II. and the Staff Manual respectively. Title pages will be prepared in manuscript.

(Erase heading not required.)

Place	Date	Hour	Summary of Events and Information	Remarks and references to Appendices
			and the Battalion was placed at the disposal of stations at H.Q. central.	
		8 p.m.	The Battalion was placed at the disposal of 71st I.B. with no idea of reorganising the Kensingtons on C.29.C.7.d. which was reported to have been broken. A.O.C. 71st I.B. however did not require the Battalion. About 6 casualties were caused by shell fire in this position. At 1 a.m. was succeeded in the new area about 4-30 a.m. Kanagoro" moved to the old front front line (25.15.L) in F94B2W6.	
I.10.central	Sept 24/16	1 a.m.	Battalion was placed at disposal of 16th I.B. and moved guided by an F.F. officer of the 6th Division to a position about I.10.central and Major Trew went to 18th I.B. H.Q. F.17.a.5.8. Orders were not given to remain in this position	
I.10.a.9.7		5.30 a.m.	for the day but were cancelled about 30 minutes later as follows:— Two companies (A+C) dug & reorganised in line from about I.10.b.central - I.11.central. One company (B) took up a position from N.W. corner of CHAUFOURS WOOD to I.12.c.5.8. The remaining company (D) moved to a dug-out in the sunken road I.12.a.9.7. Batt. H.Q. was established in the same sunken road at about I.12.a.9.7. Owing to a very heavy barrage on the sunken road notice D Coy & Batt. H.Q. entered it some 15 or 20 casualties were caused.	

WAR DIARY
or
INTELLIGENCE SUMMARY.

(Erase heading not required.)

Army Form C. 2118.

No. 3.

Instructions regarding War Diaries and Intelligence Summaries are contained in F. S. Regs., Part II. and the Staff Manual respectively. Title pages will be prepared in manuscript.

Place	Date	Hour	Summary of Events and Information	Remarks and references to Appendices
			D Coy was placed at the disposal of the O.C. 11th Essex Regt to counter attack and retake the sunken line if required.	
			The Battalion had then come under the orders of the 7th I.B.	
I.17.a.5.8.		12.30am	Batt. H.Q. moved back to the old Batt. H.Q. at I.17.a.5.8.	
I.14.a.9.7.		3-30am	Batt. H.Q. was again ordered to move to I.14.a.9.7. By this time D Coy had fallen up a position in advance of the sunken road in rear of Corps line with a Post in MORCHIES.	
I.17.a.5.8.		3-30am	The enemy broke through the Corps line in C.28.7.29. to the North of	
		5.2am	MARICOURT WOOD and at about 5-am a counter attack delivered by an infantry "B & C" Coys followed by the tanks, for about 300 yards such followed by infantry, moving forward on their flanks served to throw original position. The enemy broke through the Corps line on the flanks of the 57th Division and entered the sunken road at about I.14.b.7.4. Batt. H.Q. together with the Batt. H.Q. of the 7th Gordon Highlanders and 11th Essex was thereupon heavy machine gun fire to the H.Q. in I.17.a.5.8.	
		7.30am	Later then dies D Coy. who were still holding on in front of MORCHIES were withdrawn.	

No. 4.

Army Form C. 2118.

WAR DIARY
or
INTELLIGENCE SUMMARY.

(Erase heading not required.)

Place	Date	Hour	Summary of Events and Information	Remarks and references to Appendices
			to a position about T.17.C. "B" Coy also withdrew slightly to conform with	
			D Coy and the 11th Lanc. Fusiliers on the right.	
			B.C. Major of the 7th mixed Batt. H.Q. and gave orders for A & B Coys to	
	23/3/18	1.45am	relieve 2 Coys of 3rd Wheatstone Regt. who were holding a line T.17.a.5.8.10	
			BEET ROOT FACTORY T.17.d.5.7. A & C Coys were relieved by A & B Coys. XI QUEENS.	
			41st Division.	
			Estimated casualties up to this time 80 O.R.	
		8 a.m.	At about 8 a.m. the enemy reached his attack from CHAUFOURS WOOD to the S.E.	
			also between BOIS DE VAULX and MARICOURT WOOD. All attacks during the morning	
			were held North of the BAPAUME CAMBRAI road, but on the South of this road	
			the 51st Div & 19th Divisions were forced to withdraw which left the flank of	
			this Battalion exposed, and a defensive flank was formed along the BAPAUME	
			CAMBRAI road facing S.E.	
		3 p.m.	At about 3 p.m. 2 Battalions of the 41st Div. who were on the left of this	
			Battalion were ordered to withdraw about about 3.30 p.m. These two	
			Battalions and also the two battalions of the 19th Div. who were in the vicinity	

WAR DIARY
or
INTELLIGENCE SUMMARY.
(Erase heading not required.)

Army Form C. 2118.

No. 5.

Place	Date	Hour	Summary of Events and Information	Remarks and references to Appendices
			were ordered to withdraw forthwith.	
		3.30 am	A conference was held between the 5 Battalion commanders as to whether it was possible to withdraw 5 Battalions from a forward slope in daylight, and it was eventually decided to hang on until 6 am and then to attack BEUGNY and fight a way through to the Army line.	
		About 4.30 am	information was received from our light company that the enemy was working methodically in large numbers through the Eastern edge of BEUGNY and had already crossed the BEUGNY-MORCHIES road. It was therefore decided to withdraw to the Army line by J.Y. 200 of BEUGNY forthwith.	
G.23.d		5.15 am	The Battalion assembled in the Sunken line (Total Strength 3 Off. 81 O.R.) when orders were received to return to the transport lines near BIHUCOURT.	
		G.22.b	which were reached about 12 M.N.	
			Estimated casualties 17 Off. 419. O.R.	
			Transport had moved to this position 24 hours earlier from FAVREUIL.	
SAPIGNIES	24.3.16	1.30 pm	The Battalion rested here until 1.30 am when it ordered to take up a position with the remainder of the 75th I.B. to the E. of SAPIGNIES at about X.9.a v C.	

Army Form C. 2118.

No. 6.

WAR DIARY
or
INTELLIGENCE SUMMARY.
(Erase heading not required.)

Instructions regarding War Diaries and Intelligence Summaries are contained in F.S. Regs., Part II. and the Staff Manual respectively. Title pages will be prepared in manuscript.

Place	Date	Hour	Summary of Events and Information	Remarks and references to Appendices
			where 'B' teams rejoined the Battalion and Lt. Col. A. DARWELL. M.C. resumed command. Total strength 10 Offs. 198. O.R.	
		7.15 pm	The Battalion sent up a garrison after dark. 2 Coys about H.Q.a.8.5. and 2 Coys. who were guarded forward at request of B.B. O.'s 124 + 124 I.B. at about H.Q.d.1.7. The enemy was at this time in FAYREUIL and there were a large number of our troops belonging to 40th, 41st and 19th Divisions dugouts in this vicinity.	
LOEAST WOOD	26/3/18	3 am.	A Brigade of the 42nd Division came up and relieved the 75th Brigade group which was withdrawn to a line N.E. of LOEAST WOOD A.26.d - B.3.a. which was dug by the Brigade. Rep. Mar. 57.D. Transport had moved to LOEAST CAMP. F.30.a. (57.D.) at about N.N. 24/25th and had had to abandon at R.22.d. all blankets, packs, tent equipments and drums. A hot breakfast was given to the men in this position. During the day the Battalion was subjected to light shelling and about 6 slight casualties were caused.	

WAR DIARY or INTELLIGENCE SUMMARY

Army Form C. 2118.

No. 7.

Instructions regarding War Diaries and Intelligence Summaries are contained in F. S. Regs., Part II. and the Staff Manual respectively. Title pages will be prepared in manuscript.

(Erase heading not required.)

Place	Date	Hour	Summary of Events and Information	Remarks and references to Appendices
PUISIEUX			At about 4-30 a.m. a tank counter attack was made through the Battalion in direction of BIHUCOURT which was held by the enemy.	
		7.a.m.	At about 7 a.m. orders were received to take up a position in L.30.d + Z.31.a the S.E. of PUISIEUX. 3 companies which had moved to about F.26.c. was ordered	
	26/3/18	2.a.m.	to move to COLINCAMPS. The Battalion reached PUISIEUX about 2 a.m. + had just had a hot meal and were preparing to bedding up their position when orders were received to concentrate at BOMMECOURT.	
BOMMECOURT		5.a.m.	The Battalion reached BOMMECOURT about 5 a.m. and formed up on the valley E.26.c. where our Coys went out in protection.	
		9.a.m.	The Battalion took up a position in E.29.c. facing East.	
		12.Noon	At about 12 Noon the enemy was reported to be attacking through HEBUTERNE Northwards and the Battalion was ordered to take up a line in K.3.a + d. facing S.W. This report proved to be entirely false + the Battalion was stopped before arrival at this position and assembled in the original position E.25.c. where they remained until about 4 p.m.	
		4.p.m.	The Batt. moved and took up a line in E.22.d. facing E. and dug in.	

WAR DIARY
or
INTELLIGENCE SUMMARY.
(Erase heading not required.)

Army Form C. 2118.

No. 6.

Place	Date	Hour	Summary of Events and Information	Remarks and references to Appendices
			The transport had assembled in FONQUEVILLERS in the early morning and about midday during the above marched to ST AMAND	
		11·15 pm	Orders were received to move forthwith to COUIN. The Battalion marched off	
	27/3/18	at 12·5 am	and reached ST LEGER about 7 am where they were billeted.	
		2 pm	The Battalion marched to PUCHEVILLERS arriving about 8 pm and bivouacked in a field in N. 26. C.	
	28/3/18	7 am	The Battalion marched from PUCHEVILLERS via TALMAS - CANAPLES - DOMART to FRANQUEVILLE where it was billeted. During the period 26th - 28th the Battalion marched a distance of 38 miles. During the whole period the Battalion dug in on no less than 6 occasions. The Battalion remained at FRANQUEVILLE until 3/4 the time being spent in general organization.	
	3/3/18		The Battalion marched via BERNEUIL - FIENVILLERS - HEM to DOULLENS and entrained for RODENAERSVELDE.	

T.2134. Wt. W708-776. 50C000. 4/15. Sir J. C. & S.

Army Form C. 2118.

WAR DIARY
or
INTELLIGENCE SUMMARY.
(Erase heading not required.)

Instructions regarding War Diaries and Intelligence Summaries are contained in F. S. Regs., Part II. and the Staff Manual respectively. Title pages will be prepared in manuscript.

Place	Date	Hour	Summary of Events and Information	Remarks and references to Appendices
			Strength at beginning of month = 43 Officers 971 o.R.	
			" " end " " = 26 " 835 "	
			Casualties during month = *17 " 412 "	
			*{ Capt. Rev. B. Nicholson M.C. (W) Wounded & to England (W)	
			" A. V. Leonard M.C. (W) " J.C. Lugg (W)	
			Lieut. N.A. Williams M.C. (M) " G.J. Foster (M)	
			" E.C. Dixon (M) Lieut. W.M. Barry (M)	
			2nd Lt. J.W. Booth (M) 2nd Lt. R.W. Brown (M)	
			" R.W. Dutton (M) " E.L. Poole (M)	
			" F.J. Hayes (M) " N. Bryden (M)	
			" A.L. Kinnock (M) " G.J. Skyggs (M)	
			" M.R. Jones (M)	
			Officers leaving for other reasons:- {2nd Lieut. C.S. Taylor - sick to England; Major N. Stephens M.C. to England on duty ;	
			Capt. P.B. Gilbert - to England on duty.	
			*{ Major Bedern	
			*{ Capt. G.R. Barton	
			Drafts during month :- *2 Officers 318 o.R.	
			Stancell	
			Lieut Col,	
			Comdg. 11th (S) Derbyshire Regiment.	

25th Division.
75th Infantry Brigade.

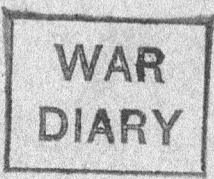

11th BATTALION

THE CHESHIRE REGIMENT

APRIL 1918

Army Form C. 2118.

WAR DIARY
or
INTELLIGENCE SUMMARY.
(Erase heading not required.)

11th Bn Cheshire Regt

Place	Date	Hour	Summary of Events and Information	Remarks and references to Appendices
	1-4-18		The Battalion detrained at GODEWAERSVELDE and was moved by bus to KORTEPYP No 2 CAMP. Sheet 28.T.26.b.5.5.	
	3.4.18		The Battalion marched to INGERSOLL CAMP (Sh 36 B.10.c.) where a draft of 260 R. was received.	
	6.4.18		The Battalion marched to LE ROSSIGNOL CAMP Sh.36 B.10.d.9.7. in Brigade Reserve	
	8.4.18		On the night of the 8th the Battalion relieved the 2nd SOUTH LANCASHIRE REGT. in the line from U.22.a.5.6. to U.28.a.6.1.	
	9/4/18		The Battalion held the line on the South side of PLOEGSTEERT WOOD.	
	9/4/18		ditto	
	10/4/18		The enemy bombarded the front and support line and all the back areas which increased with intensity up to 5.30 am, when news came that the enemy was in LE TOUQUET STATION. At about 5.50 am the enemy was seen attacking up our flank coming from the South. At the same time parties of the enemy were seen in rear of Battalion Headquarters which caused H.Q. to withdraw, and they went out in the direction of PLOEGSTEERT WOOD being fired at the whole time from the direction of LANCASHIRE SUPPORT FARM and on passing	

PLOEGSTEERT VILLAGE hostile of enemy French machine guns. Lieut Col. G. Danwell M.C. was hit whilst withdrawing his Rearguards and the command passed to Major S. Trevor D.S.O. M.C. who had gone to Brigade to give them the situation. Officers were then sent for us to form a line in rear of the 2nd & 5th LANCS BATT. nohich the PLOEGSTEERT - ROMARIN ROAD. (Sheet 28. T. 29. d. 9. 7.). This line was held until mid day. the 11th. The Battalion then took up a position on the right of the 2nd South Lancashire Regiment facing South and at 12 mid day, the whole line was attacked and driven back to the Army line. We held the line on the East side of the ROMARIN - NEUVE EGLISE road. Orders came that the right flank of the Battalion on our right was in a dangerous position so we were called out to form a defensive flank along the KOETEPYP ROAD (T.27.a. and b.) but shortly after the situation cleared up and we took up our position (T.21.d.7.) again on the Army line. At 7pm the Battalion moved to PONT D'ACHELLES to dig a line from ROMARIN to PONT D'ACHELLE. This line was started on, but finding the enemy were in the occupation of ROMARIN a line was dug about 200 yards in rear of the ROMARIN - PONT D'ACHELLE, and

Army Form C. 2118.

WAR DIARY
or
INTELLIGENCE SUMMARY.
(Erase heading not required.)

Instructions regarding War Diaries and Intelligence Summaries are contained in F. S. Regs., Part II. and the Staff Manual respectively. Title pages will be prepared in manuscript.

Place	Date	Hour	Summary of Events and Information	Remarks and references to Appendices
			occupied until 4pm 12th with the 9TH CHESHIRE on our right, 6TH. SOUTH WALES BORDERS on our left, and the 8TH BORDERS in support.	
	12/4/18		The enemy attacked this position at 4pm and we were forced to withdraw to the KEETEPYP road (T.27 a and b) where we dug in for the night.	
	13/4/18		At 5AM on the 13th the enemy attacked again and we had to withdraw to the line at RAVELSBURG (Sheet 28. S.18. D. 8. 5) which we held until relieved.	
	14/4/18		The enemy tried an attack on the 14th but was repulsed by artillery and machine gun fire.	
	15/4/18		On the 15th April at 3.30 am we were relieved by the 2ND LEICESTERS and marched to DRANOUTRE (S.5. B. 9. 5) where we stopped until 2pm and then marched to camp on the MONT DES CATS - GODERSVELDE road (Sheet 27. R.19 a 5.2.)	
	16/4/18		On this date the Brigade formed a composite battalion and went into the line (Sheet 28. M.25. d. 5. 5) under orders of the 7th Brigade.	
	18/4/18		The composite Battalion came out of the line and we went back to the camp on the MONT=DES CATS - GODERSVELDE road (Sh. 27. R.19.a.5.2).	

Army Form C. 2118.

WAR DIARY
or
INTELLIGENCE SUMMARY.
(Erase heading not required.)

Instructions regarding War Diaries and Intelligence Summaries are contained in F.S. Regs., Part II. and the Staff Manual respectively. Title pages will be prepared in manuscript.

Place	Date	Hour	Summary of Events and Information	Remarks and references to Appendices
R.27.a.5.y.	19.4.18 20.4.18		Training in this camp.	
	21.4.18		Marched to F. Camp PESELHOEK (Sheet	
	22.4.18 23.4.18 24.4.18		Training in this camp.	
	25.4.18		Marched to concentration area in RENINGHELST (Sheet 28.G.2.2.6).	
	26.4.18		Marched to NEWCASTLE CAMP (G35.c.6.5) and about 2pm received orders to form a	
	27.4.18		defensive flank on high ground North of LA CLYTTE (Sh 28. N.1.c). and at 5pm we went back to NEWCASTLE CAMP	
		At 4pm	the Battalion went into support and relieved the 7th Brigade.	
		At 10pm	the Battalion relieved the 11TH LANCS FUSILIERS in support (N.7.B and D) the Brigade having taken over the line.	
	28.4.18		Quiet.	
	29.4.18		Heavy shelling the whole day. Front and support lines were frequently barraged but no enemy attack developed.	
	30.4.18		Quiet	
	31.4.18 1.5.18		The Battalion was relieved by the 10TH CHESHIRES at 10pm and moved back to BLACKBURN CAMP (G35.d.5.5)	

WAR DIARY
or
INTELLIGENCE SUMMARY.
(Erase heading not required.)

Army Form C. 2118.

Place	Date	Hour	Summary of Events and Information	Remarks and references to Appendices
	3.5.18		Battalion came out of the line and marched to ST ELOI CAMP (She. 27. K.2. 9a)	
			Strength at beginning of month. 25 Offs. 653 OR	
			" " end " 24 " 597 "	
			Drafts during month. *15 " 492 "	
			Casualties during month. *18 " 662 "	

Died from wounds:
- 2 Lt Richards
- " J. Curtis
- " J. P. Roberts
- " R. Boorquin
- " R. T. King
- " Lt F. M. Hanson

Wounded:
- 2 Lt Davies
- " Cuthbertson
- " W. Barrow
- " G. Hopwood
- " G. M. James
- " J. Rosebuck
- " Rustowski

Kept at Army M.C.
2nd Lt A. Taylor
" F. Hammond
" L. Thomas
" J. Woodward
" D. O'Toole
Case of Concussion M.C.
2nd Lt J. Bostrom
" M. Curtis

Cas J. Schofer
" Col. R. Mace
2nd Lt A. Meyer
Lieut F. D. Thorne
2nd Lt G. V. Harvey
Lieut G. F. Harvey
Capt G. R. Barton
2nd Lt R. O. Gray
" E. W. E. Allen

[signature]
Lieut Col.
Comdg 11th (S) Bn Cheshire Regt.

11 Cheshire Rgt

WAR DIARY
or
INTELLIGENCE SUMMARY.
(Erase heading not required.)

Army Form C. 2118.

VOL 30

Place	Date	Hour	Summary of Events and Information	Remarks and references to Appendices
	1/5/18		The Battalion was relieved in the line by the 10th S. Batt. Cheshire Regiment and moved into Divisional Reserve, where it remained until the 3rd.	
	3/5/18		Moved to VOT VERLE and PESSELHOCK.	
	4-7/5		Marched to HERZEELE and remained in billets until the 7th. During this period Battalion and Company training was carried out.	
	8-10/5		The Battalion entrained at about midday of the 10th.	
	10-23/5		The Battalion was billeted in MONT SUR COURVILLE where training was carried on.	Jan. FISMES arrived there
	23-26/5		On the night of the 23rd. The Battalion marched via ST PIERRE — FISMES — COURLANDON to billets in ROMAIN. On the night of the 26th. marched to VENTELAY.	
	27/5		Moved to CONCEVREUX.	
	28-31/5		The Battalion went in action during the enemy attacks on the AISNE and the MARNE. On the 29th/5 Lieut. Col. E. BROS DSO MC	

Army Form C. 2118.

WAR DIARY
or
INTELLIGENCE SUMMARY.
(Erase heading not required.)

Instructions regarding War Diaries and Intelligence Summaries are contained in F. S. Regs., Part II. and the Staff Manual respectively. Title pages will be prepared in manuscript.

Place	Date	Hour	Summary of Events and Information	Remarks and references to Appendices
			was wounded and the command of the Battalion was taken over by Capt. H.M. WILKINSON, R.C. who was killed on the following day. Major A.W. ROBINSON then assumed command of the Battalion	
			Drafts received during month 15 Officers 302 O.R.	
			" " " " 18 " 451 "	
			Casualties	
				A. Watts
				Major
				Comdg. 1/5th Can. Electric Regt.

[top left annotation:] Lt Col
11/Cheshire
May 1918

1·ORMONDE·TERRACE·
·N·W·3·
·PRIMROSE·5266·

5th May 1931

Dear Sir,

Your Reference 1918/A.

I regret the delay in replying to your letter of 22nd April but I am no longer living at 27, Marlborough Hill.

I am afraid that after this lapse of time my memory of the events of May 1918 is not very good. Col: Prior was wounded in the afternoon of 27th May and I myself was knocked out and left as dead shortly after dawn on the 28th after which I have no personal knowledge of what happened but I imagine the remnants of the Battalion were amalgamated with the 6th Bn: The Cheshire Regt before the end of the Aisne fighting.

If it would be of any use I should be happy to call upon you and endeavour to indicate the movements of the Battalion on the 27th and night of the 27/28th, but without a map I should not like to attempt to give any statement.

I am at present working at the Middlesex Hospital and can always be obtained on the telephone there (Museum 1056) during office hours.

Yours faithfully

H. L. Wilkinson

The Director,
Historical Section (Military Branch).

Army Form C. 2118.

11 Cheshire Regt
T.C.
vol 31

WAR DIARY
or
INTELLIGENCE SUMMARY.
(Erase heading not required.)

Instructions regarding War Diaries and Intelligence Summaries are contained in F. S. Regs., Part II. and the Staff Manual respectively. Title pages will be prepared in manuscript.

Place	Date	Hour	Summary of Events and Information	Remarks and references to Appendices
	7th – 8th June 1916		The Battalion, with the exception of a few officers and men who were in the line with composite Battalions, were billetted at LOISY EN BRIE where it remained under the O.R. Major L.J. Bridges Newcastle Regiment, assumed command of the Battalion.	
	14th June		On this date the Battalion formed part of the 75th Composite Battalion under the command of Lieut. Col. Mather 2nd South Lancashire Regiment	
	16th		Major W.G. Newth, Gloucestr Regt. took over command of the Battalion from Major J.C. Bridges who proceeded to command the 1st Wiltshire Regt.	
	17th – 18th		The Battalion moved to the STT LOUP area and remained there until the 15th. During the period general training was carried out. On the 11th the Divisional Commander inspected the Battalion. On the 17th instant the remaining portion of the Battalion was relieved in the line by Italian troops. On the 18th the Battalion, with the exception of the Training Staff, was absorbed by the 1/6 Battalion Cheshire Regt.	
	19th – 23rd		The 11th Battalion the New Regimental Training Staff entrained at CONNANTRE proceeding to join the 39th Division and arrived at ZOUARQUES on the 23rd.	
	24th 25th – 30th		The Training Staff took over the supervision of the training of the 1st and 3rd Battalions 118th Infantry Regiment, American Expeditionary Force and commenced duties from the 25th to the 30th.	

Strength of Staff = 8 Officers – 37 OR.

A.W. Robinson Major.
Commdg. 11th Battalion Cheshire Regt.

T.C. 11 Cheshire R.

Army Form C. 2118.

WAR DIARY
or
INTELLIGENCE SUMMARY.
(Erase heading not required) (11th/16 Bn)   Vol 32

Instructions regarding War Diaries and Intelligence Summaries are contained in F. S. Regs., Part II. and the Staff Manual respectively. Title pages will be prepared in manuscript.

Place	Date	Hour	Summary of Events and Information	Remarks and references to Appendices
	1/7/18.		The Battalion was attached to the 1st & 3rd Batts. 118th American Regiments for instructional purposes.	
	2/7/18		The 30th American Division moved to Quatorpe Reserve, the 1st & 3rd Batts 118th Regiment were accompanied by 3 Officers (Commanding Officer and two Company Commanders) from the Battalion for instructional purposes. These officers returned to the Battalion on the 19th July.	
	2nd to 30/7/18.		The Battalion carried on General and Recreational training.	
			Strength at beginning of month. 8 Officers 36 O.R.	
			Draft received during month. - 2 O.R.	
			Strength at end of month. 8 Officers 38 O.R.	

A.W. Robinson Major
Commanding 11th Bn Cheshire Regt